Keep Cookin' Cowgirl

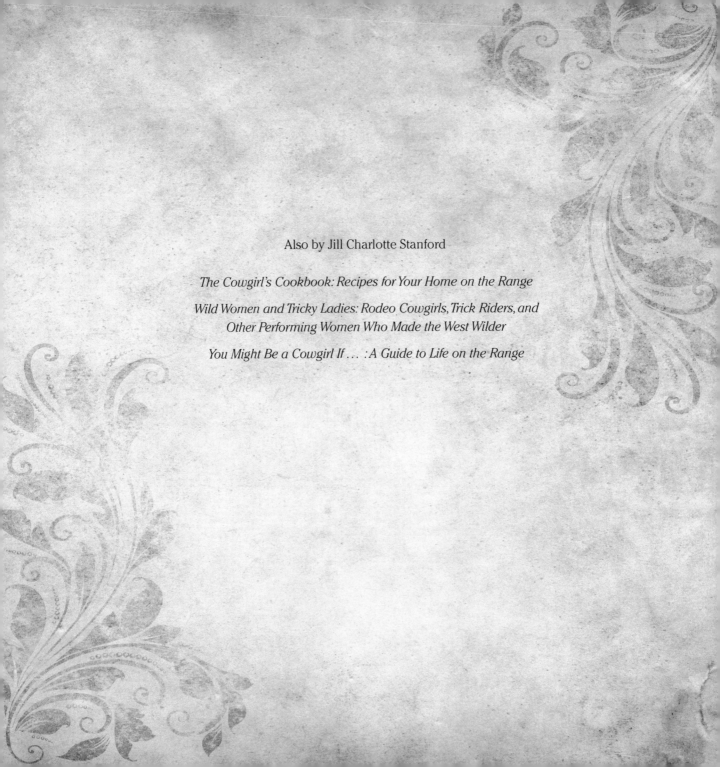

Also by Jill Charlotte Stanford

The Cowgirl's Cookbook: Recipes for Your Home on the Range

*Wild Women and Tricky Ladies: Rodeo Cowgirls, Trick Riders, and
Other Performing Women Who Made the West Wilder*

You Might Be a Cowgirl If … : A Guide to Life on the Range

Keep Cookin' Cowgirl

MORE RECIPES FOR YOUR HOME ON THE RANGE

JILL CHARLOTTE STANFORD

Author of *The Cowgirl's Cookbook*

TWODOT®

GUILFORD, CONNECTICUT
HELENA, MONTANA

AN IMPRINT OF GLOBE PEQUOT PRESS

A · **TWODOT**® · **BOOK**

Copyright © 2013 by Jill Charlotte Stanford

ALL RIGHTS RESERVED. No part of this book may be reproduced or transmitted in any form by any means, electronic or mechanical, including photocopying and recording, or by any information storage and retrieval system, except as may be expressly permitted in writing from the publisher. Requests for permission should be addressed to Globe Pequot Press, Attn: Rights and Permissions Department, PO Box 480, Guilford, CT 06437.

TwoDot is an imprint of Globe Pequot Press and a registered trademark of Morris Book Publishing, LLC.

Project editor: Lauren Brancato
Text design and layout: Sue Murray

Library of Congress Cataloging-in-Publication data is available on file.

ISBN 978-0-7627-8832-3

Printed in the United States of America

10 9 8 7 6 5 4 3 2

Contents

AUTHOR'S COLLECTION

Acknowledgments

This photograph taken by Ralph Russell Doubleday around 1925 of relay riders Mabel Strickland, Vera McGinnis, Mona Cowan, and Josephine Wicks sums up how I picture my friends who have helped *Keep Cookin' Cowgirl* reach the finish line.

In a relay race, the first rider mounts her excited horse (this is no easy feat in itself) and sprints away from the starting line with a baton in her hand. She gallops like the wind around the arena and hands the baton off to the next, waiting cowgirl, who charges away and around; this rider hands it to the next rider, who tears around as fast as she can to the next and last rider. The handoff is made without dropping the baton (this wastes precious time), and the final horse and rider hightails it around the dirt track and crosses the line, grinning from ear to ear as she leaps off her lathered horse. Teamwork, skill, and the ability to focus are all important if you are going to win the race.

I felt very much like the starting relay rider when Erin Turner, my esteemed editor at TwoDot, called me and told me the publishers wanted a brand-new *Cowgirl's Cookbook,* in a very short period of time. She asked, "Can you do it?" The track looked long and the winning time had to be fast, but I had a feeling there would be Cowgirls lined up and waiting to grab the baton from my hand and whirl away to the finish line, allowing me to win the race.

My deepest thanks go to my Facebook friends and Cowgirls, ranch wives, trick riders, and horse trainers. This book is dedicated to all of you who saddled right up and galloped to me with a wonderful recipe straight from your kitchen. Your commitment to helping me was stellar. Some of you I will never meet face to face. A few of you I have had the extreme pleasure of giving a hug to and sharing laughter with, already old friends even though we had just met. I feel as if we all know each other very well. We have been on roundups; brandings; weddings; births of baby girls and boys, foals, calves, lambs, puppies, and kittens; blizzards; snowstorms; heat waves; ill parents; grandchildren's triumphs; road trips; stepping on a colt for the first time; and posting about it with joy because all the hard work paid off and no one got bucked off.

Many times my friends got out their cameras or iPhones and snapped pictures of the territory they were riding in to share with the rest of us. This is a vast and beautiful land, and Cowgirls see it best from the top of a horse.

This is what one of my Facebook friends said: "I hate to admit it, but I LOVE Facebook. I get to visit with other women with the same interests as myself." That's how I feel, too. These friends are always here for me, and I am here for them. We share life's joys and pleasures, mourn the sadness that can fall, send our thoughts and wishes to one another, and throughout it all, we are bound together as Cowgirls!

So Gals, this one's for you!

My deepest thanks to: Ginnie Bakersfield; Demetra Bell-Runnels; Adrianne Brockman; Rosemary Browne; Barb Carr; Mackenzie Carr, Miss Rodeo USA 2012; Nicole Carter; Audrey Clossen; Claudia Conger; Jennifer J. Denison; Donna Higby; Starr Emmings; Hildy Larson; June Lee; Marti Lee; Caprice Madison, aka Mountain Woman; Lindsey Martinez; Jan Mendoza; Fran Rattay; Peggy Veach-Robinson; Marjorie Rogers; Charmain Vaughn; and Blair Woodfield.

Special thanks go to my sister, Robin Johnson. Robin is a retired culinary educator, and she enthusiastically saddled up and brought in the strays. She cooked and photographed many of the recipes for me. I am very grateful for her help.

I would also like to thank Ted Moomaw from the Old Bucking Horse Museum; Lori Bright from Hamley Steakhouse, Pendleton, Oregon; Jen Dibbern of the Colorado Historical Society; Coi Drummond-Gerhrig of the Denver Library Archives; and Caitlin Vargas for Pendleton Whisky.

Preface: Back on the Range

A list of the Top 25 American Comfort Foods was published recently. It should come as no surprise that more than half of the good things on that list appear right here in *Keep Cookin' Cowgirl* and the other half was in my first book, *The Cowgirl's Cookbook*.

Cowgirls have always known what makes a person happy, and that is good food, prepared simply. If you are getting ready to go out on a dark and frosty morning, you will welcome a hot breakfast that will stick to your ribs. Sunday supper has long been a tradition on the ranch—a time when folks can get together and discuss the week behind and the week ahead while enjoying a warm meal around the table. Special occasions, like a wedding or a birthday, are celebrated with something homemade. Often, it will be a potluck where everybody's best recipe gets to shine and be enjoyed. Campfire cooking, which started out of necessity when large herds of cattle were being moved and the chuck wagon was the kitchen, holds a special place in the hearts of those lucky enough to have eaten under the stars.

I've had a wonderful time putting this new cookbook together, kitchen-testing some new and really delightful dishes from all over the United States. Along the way, I've gotten to know better many of the Cowgirls who participated with me. It's been said that Cowgirls cook with three

ingredients: salt, pepper, and catsup. Almost true! There are no "bouquets garnis" in Cowgirl cooking.

I do not apologize for the ingredients you will find here. Yes, there are "cream of" soups, prepared mixes, and tubes of biscuits. Many of the cooks who contributed these recipes live far, far out and away from a handy grocery store in case they run out of something. They know and appreciate the convenience of prepared mixes and cans, to say nothing of the shelf life. It's what they do with these things that makes these recipes special.

There are a few more "Desserts and Sweets" in this book than the first one because, well, who doesn't like something sweet, sticky, gooey, or all three and then some? It's the reward at the end of the day.

I've added some recipes for cooking game, both feathered and furred. "Camping Out" is another addition, and it is an old tradition. Heck, not so very long ago, cooking over a fire was the only way dinner or breakfast was cooked out on the range.

You will notice a few of the recipes just could not be put into "standard recipe form." They are best prepared if you read the instruction out loud, because that Cowgirl is standing right there next to you, urging you along. An example: I am not a good baker. Yeast and I do not see eye-to-eye. However, Marti Lee wrote me a foolproof recipe in her

ROBIN L. COREY

distinctive Mississippi voice for yeast rolls, and by golly, they turned out perfectly because I could hear her telling me just how to do it.

Always trust a Cowgirl. That's the most important lesson I learned. They shoot straight and they never lie. They become your BFF in a hurry. And boy, can they whip up a meal at a gallop and make it look easy!

It's been a pleasure, believe me.

Jill Charlotte Stanford
Sisters, Oregon

Cowgirls and Cooking

by Jessica Hedges

*Now as long as there have been cowboys, there have
been cowgirls there to cook
From dude ranches to cow camps, pack stations to
ranch houses they were there
Sometimes they cook from memory, other times they
adapt from a book
But you know that each meal prepared is made with
love and blessed with a prayer.*

*When the evening chores are complete and the cavvy
turned out to graze
She sets into the kitchen to fix a meal after her long
day's ride
For this extra work she does not expect wealth, nor
does she expect praise
But she looks forward to another sunrise that she can
face with pride.*

*For by the time sunrise comes, she will have been
awake for several hours
Rolling biscuits out hot and flakey like her mother had
done before
Taught from a child the secrets of a cast-iron skillet's
powers
There'll be a spread that every cowboy in the county
will come beg for.*

*And so begins another day of dust and sweat, rawhide
and leather
With simple but hearty food to fuel a body through the
work ahead
Just like a cowboy would ride through hell, he would
ride through any weather
There will be a woman, called a cowgirl, with hot
coffee and fresh baked bread.*

PHOTO BY BECKY KINGEN, FLYING K CUSTOM COWBOYING, AND USED WITH THE PERMISSION OF JESSICA HEDGES

Jessica is a cowgirl poet living in Idaho with her Buckaroo husband, Sam, and their young son, Quirt. She is the winner of the 2010 Academy of Western Artists Cowboy Poetry CD of the Year, the 2010 Academy of Western Artists top 5 finalists for Female Poet of the Year, and the 2010 Columbia River Cowboy Gathering People's Choice Award Winner.

Visit Jessica on her website, www.jessicahedges cowboypoetry.com, where she lists her CDs and writes a blog about being a poet and a ranch wife.

We cowgirls have butted in on a so-called strictly man's game—and if to "play" on the hurricane deck on a sun-fishin', whirlly-giggin', rearin'-up, fallin'-over-backward, squallin', bitin', strikin', buckin', roman-nosed cayuse ain't a he-man's game, there never will be one—still, as I say, we cowgirls that like the game well enough to play it should play it just like the cowboys do. Why, I'd feel insulted . . . if I was told to tie my stirrups down!

—Bonnie McCarroll

Beverages

On a hot prairie day or a cold northern night with the snow falling silently outside, or following a hard day's work in the saddle, you will find the perfect beverage here.

GLENBOW ARCHIVES #3930-2

Cowgirl's Tea

This recipe, sometimes called "Russian Tea," has been around for a very long time. It was first served to me by Adrianne Brockman. She rode hunters and jumpers, showed a beautiful black Arabian horse in a variety of Western classes, and was the only woman on the Lake Oswego Hunt Club Polo Team. A Real Cowgirl!

You can adjust the ingredients to your own personal tastes. I know one Cowgirl who puts the candy Red Hots (about a quarter cup) into the mix. "Spices it up," she says.

Makes 40 servings

2 cups powdered Tang
1 cup powdered instant tea
1 cup sweetened lemonade mix
1 teaspoon ground cloves
1 teaspoon ground cinnamon
2 cups sugar

Combine all the ingredients in a large bowl and mix well. Put the mixture into a large jar and seal tightly.

To serve, put 2 teaspoons (or more) of the mix into a cup and add boiling water. You can put a drop or two of whiskey in your cup if it's been a long day.

Divide this mixture into smaller Mason jars, tie a bit of raffia around the lid, and give as a winter gift.

You don't win buckles for a clean house.

—Anonymous

Cowpuncher's Punch

After a hot day out on the range, a glass or two of cold, old-fashioned Cowpuncher's Punch will wet yer whistle.

Makes 24 servings

    4 cups stewed black tea, cold
    4 cups orange juice
    4 lemons, squeezed
    4 oranges, thinly sliced
    1 cup sugar
    16 cups cracked ice
    12 cups ginger ale
    4 cups soda water or sparkling water
    1 bunch fresh mint for garnish

Combine tea, juices, orange slices, and sugar. Stir until the sugar dissolves. Chill.

Put cracked ice in a tall, 8-ounce glass. Fill the glass halfway with the tea mix. Add the ginger ale and soda water just before serving. Garnish with fresh mint, if available.

Want to get real fancy if this is for a party? Make an ice ring in that old Jell-O mold you kept, filled with more orange and lemon slices, mint leaves, and maraschino cherries. Unmold it into the punch bowl filled with the tea mixture, and garner compliments.

GLENBOW ARCHIVES #NA-365-1

Mexican Hot Chocolate

Even grown-up Cowgirls need marshmallows in their hot chocolate and maybe just a little bit of spice.

Makes 3 servings

> 3–4 tablespoons granulated sugar
> 3 tablespoons baking cocoa
> ¼ teaspoon ground cinnamon
> ½ teaspoon chili powder
> 2⅓ cups milk
> ½ teaspoon vanilla extract
> 1 marshmallow per serving, or more . . .

Combine the sugar, cocoa, cinnamon, and chili powder in a small, heavy-duty saucepan. Gradually stir in the milk. Warm over medium heat, stirring constantly, until hot (do not boil).

Remove from the heat, then stir in the vanilla extract. Beat with a wire whisk until frothy. Put a marshmallow in the bottom of each cup, divide the hot chocolate into the cups, and sprinkle a little more cinnamon on top.

It ain't braggin' if you can do it.

—Dizzy Dean

Ranch House Milkshake

A very simple recipe for a vanilla milkshake. When you add chocolate syrup, you have a chocolate milkshake. Fresh berries or fresh peaches in the summer are wonderful, and crushed peppermint candies during the holidays is quite festive. Just try not to spill the milk.

Makes 2 milkshakes

> 2 cups vanilla ice cream
> 1 cup 2% milk
> 2 teaspoons vanilla extract

Put all the ingredients in a blender, then add your favorite flavors if you like. Blend on high for 1 minute.

Pour into tall glasses, get your straw, and go out on the porch.

COURTESY, HISTORY COLORADO #X9237

Caramel Creamer

This is so simple, and you won't have to pay the high price at the grocery store. Better yet? You can make it taste the way you like by adding more vanilla, less vanilla—you get the idea.

> 1½ cups sugar
> ½ cup water
> 1 cup heavy whipping cream
> 1 teaspoon vanilla
> 4 cups half-and-half

Mix the sugar and water in a saucepan and bring to 240°F. Remove the pan from the heat.

Using a whisk, slowly add the cream and vanilla. Add the half-and-half and whisk well.

Allow the creamer to cool completely before pouring it into a quart jar. Store in your icebox.

I discovered I was totally unsuited for the life of bridge, telephoning, socials, and social visiting. The great big world was out there and there were things to be done.

—Blanche Stuart Scott, 1910

"Cow Girls" at the Pendleton "Round Up" 1911

Rodeo Rita

In 1910 the first Pendleton Round-Up was touted as "a frontier exhibition of picturesque pastimes, Indian and military spectacles, cowboy racing and bronco busting for the championship of the Northwest." It turned out to be that and more. "The largest crowd in Pendleton's history," 7,000 strong, showed up for the first show on September 29, 1910. Round-Up remains today a strong tradition.

After a hard day in the chutes, here's a cocktail "double damn guaranteed" to cure what ails you. Made from a blended Canadian whiskey, the 80-proof oak barrel–aged whiskey uses glacier-fed springwater from Mount Hood, Oregon. It's widely known as "the Cowboy Whiskey." I would add it's a favorite among Cowgirls, too.

Makes 1 cocktail

> 1 ounce Pendleton Whisky
> 3 ounces margarita mix

For the rim:
> 1 teaspoon salt in a shallow saucer
> 2 lime wedges

Run a lime wedge around the rim of the glass, then dip it into the salt in the saucer.

Pour the Pendleton Whisky and margarita mix into a cocktail shaker filled with crushed ice. Shake and serve over ice in an 8-ounce highball glass with a salted rim.

Garnish with a lime wedge and "Let 'er buck!"

Lavender Blossom Cocktail

Sometimes, a Cowgirl wants something kinda "girlie." This ought to do the trick.

Makes 1 cocktail

> Shaved ice
> 1 jigger (1½ ounces) gin
> Dash of Lavender Simple Syrup (recipe below)
> Splash of champagne
> Fresh blueberries or lemon peel for garnish

Place the ice, gin, and lavender syrup (in that order) into a tall bar glass. Stir gently with a long-handled spoon, and top with a champagne finish.

Add a few fresh blueberries for garnish, or lemon peel cut into a fine strip.

Lavender Simple Syrup
> 1 cup sugar
> 1 cup water
> ¼ cup fresh or dried lavender blossoms

In a medium saucepan, combine the sugar and water. Bring to a boil, stirring, until sugar has dissolved.

Add the lavender blossoms. Allow to cool. Strain to remove the blossoms.

Store in the icebox in a glass container. This is also refreshing in lemonade.

Parched and Dry Rescue Potation

*"All day I've faced
The burning waste
Without a drop of water . . . "*

You can make your own rehydrating drink. Keep this in your canteen for those times you have to face the "burning waste."

Mix until dissolved:
1 quart warm water
Juice of 2–3 lemons
⅓ cup honey
½ teaspoon sea salt

Chill.

Horse's Neck

A Horse's Neck is a cocktail made with bourbon (or brandy) and ginger ale, with a long spiral of lemon peel (zest) draped over the edge of an old-fashioned or highball (8-ounce) glass, looking very much like a tired old nag's neck.

Dating back to the 1890s, the drink started out as a nonalcoholic mixture of ginger ale, ice, and lemon peel. By the 1910s, bourbon or brandy was added for a "Horse's Neck with a Kick."

Makes 1 cocktail

> 2 ounces bourbon or brandy
> 8 ounces ginger ale
> 2–3 dashes Angostura bitters (optional)
> 1 long spiral of lemon peel for garnish

Pour the bourbon or brandy and ginger ale over ice in a highball glass. Add the bitters if desired and stir gently.

Drape the lemon peel over the rim of the glass, leaving the "neck" hanging out over the edge.

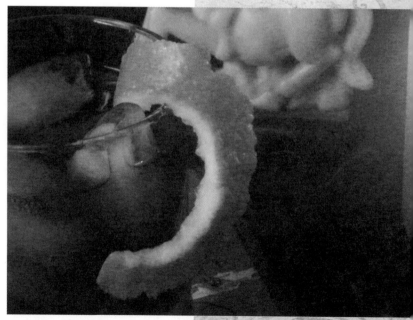

JILL CHARLOTTE STANFORD

Bertha Blancett

Long before women's lib, the fairer sex got into the act at the Pendleton Round-Up— cowgirls in the early days of the Round-Up could be as tough as the men. In 1914 Bertha Blancett, wife of cowboy Del Blancett, came within 12 points of winning the all-around title.

Tall, Dark & Hamley

Camille Woodfield, bartender, and Isis Miller, restaurant and saloon manager at the famed Hamley Steakhouse in Pendleton, Oregon—home of the Pendleton Round-Up—have concocted the most amazing cocktail using Hamley's own whiskey, the first-ever Oregon-made straight wheat whiskey on the market. Hamley Whiskey is a small-batch wheat whiskey grown, distilled, and bottled in eastern Oregon by Stein Distillery of Joseph. With its unique, more mellow taste, softer than bourbon, it delivers a smooth, high-quality cocktail without an overpowering or heavy taste experience. You will love its vibrant chestnut color, hint of brown sugar and soft oak, and warm toasted pecan finish. You will *really* like this special drink.

Makes 1 cocktail

½ ounce gin
½ ounce vodka
½ ounce rum
½ ounce triple sec
½ ounce Hamley Whiskey
Splash of sweet and sour mix
Splash of Coke
Lemon slice, lime slice, and maraschino cherry for garnish

Shake the gin, vodka, rum, triple sec, whiskey, and Sweet-n-Sour in a cocktail shaker filled with shaved ice. Pour into a 16-ounce glass and top off with a splash of Coke.

Garnish with a lemon slice, lime slice, and maraschino cherry.

Sweet and sour is a mixer and can be found in grocery stores in the beverage section for grown-ups. It does not, as I first assumed, have anything to do with Chinese cooking.

The Old-Fashioned Cowgirl Cocktail

Makes 1 cocktail

1 teaspoon sugar
Dash of bitters
2 ounces good whiskey
Splash of club soda
Maraschino cherry and
orange segment for
garnish

Put the sugar and bitters in a highball glass (8- to 12-ounce capacity) and muddle, or mash, them together. Pour in the whiskey, add 2 or 3 cubes of ice, and top with club soda.

Garnish with a maraschino cherry and an orange segment on a toothpick.

Sonora Carver

Hard to believe, just looking at the picture. The horse dived about 50 feet into a tank of water about 10 feet deep, and Miss Sonora Carver stayed on the horse the entire time, leaping onto its back and holding a special rigging at the last moment as the horse galloped up a long ramp. Sonora lost her eyesight in 1931 when her horse landed badly, but by 1932 she was again diving horses. She retired in 1942 and died in 2003 at the age of ninety-nine. There is a wonderful movie called *Wild Hearts Can't Be Broken* about her life with her amazing horses. She says in her memoirs that "the horses enjoyed doing this stunt. I never had one that wouldn't freely gallop up that ramp, pause for me to jump on and leap into space."

GLENBOW ARCHIVES #NB-16-417

Cowgirl's First Aid

Okay, you forgot to put your leather gloves on, didn't you?! Got a barbed wire cut, didn't you?! Luckily for you, if applied properly, sugar will act as a natural and fairly effective antiseptic for cuts when standard antiseptics aren't available.

For other small "owies" all you need is granulated sugar, petroleum jelly, bandage/cloth, and clean water. Small wounds, ulcerations, and sores will respond better to the use of sugar as treatment than those that are large or exceedingly deep. Sanitize the area of the wound by thoroughly washing it with clean water. Pat or air dry the area completely before moving on to the next step.

Gently apply a small amount of petroleum jelly, circling the wound but not touching it. Then sprinkle sugar onto the wound, covering it completely a bit at a time. Dress the wound with a small piece of gauze or sterile cloth and, if available, cover the wound with a bandage. If you don't have a bandage available, you can use pieces of medical tape, masking tape, or even a bit of duct tape. Keep the wound clean by changing the bandage and sugar application every twenty-four hours. This will help it heal faster, and further reduce the risk of infection.

Breakfast

In a Cowgirl's world, breakfast is the most important meal of the day. A "stick-to-your-ribs" breakfast can make a long day in the saddle a little shorter, and you can ride a little farther.

Cowgirl at Calgary Stampede. Sept. 2–7, 1912.

Breakfast Apples

A hearty breakfast is the only way to start the day out West. This easy-to-do apple dish is good on its own but even better on top of oatmeal with a little cream. Guaranteed to help you get through the branding until lunch! You can also serve this over ice cream (see page 132 for a nifty, quick way to make ice cream) back at the ranch house for dessert.

PS: Save the peelings and cores for the horses.

Serves 6

    3 tablespoons butter
    3 medium tart apples, peeled, cored, quartered, and sliced
    ⅓ cup sugar, plus 2–3 tablespoons

Melt the butter in a medium-heavy iron skillet over medium heat.

Add the apples to the skillet. Cover and cook for 5 minutes, or until the apples are juicy and browned. (If you are cooking these over a campfire, use aluminum foil for the cover.)

Turn the apples and sprinkle with the ⅓ cup of sugar. Reduce the heat to low (or move the skillet on the grill of the campfire away from direct heat).

Cover again and cook for about 5 minutes longer. Uncover and cook 2 to 3 minutes longer, or until the sugar is absorbed and the apples are lightly browned on the bottom.

Remove from the heat and sprinkle with the reserved sugar. Best served warm.

PHOTO BY ROBIN JOHNSON

Burnin' Daylight Oatmeal

"Sun's up! Strike a trot! We're burnin' daylight!" That's the traditional call of the foreman to his hands before they head out onto the range to gather cattle. On a cold and miserable morning, modern-day Cowgirls might want to serve this wonderful oatmeal devised by my personal camp cook, my sister Robin.

Serves 2–3

> 1 cup old-fashioned oats
> 1¾ cups water or milk
> Pinch of salt
> ½ cup cut-up apples or pears
> ¼ cup chopped walnuts or pecans
> ⅛ cup toasted sunflower seeds
> 2 tablespoons toasted coconut flakes
> 2 tablespoons each golden raisins, cut-up dried figs, apricots, and dates
> 1 cup warmed milk
> Brown sugar or maple syrup to taste

Make old-fashioned oats as directed on the package for the amount you want. This recipe calls for 1 cup of oats added to boiling salted water. Cook on medium-low for 5 minutes. Put a lid on the cooked oatmeal and let it rest for about 5 minutes.

Divide the oats mixture between 2 or 3 bowls. Sprinkle with the apples or pears (or a mixture of both), walnuts or pecans, sunflower seeds, coconut flakes, and dried fruit. Pour some warmed milk into each bowl, and top with either brown sugar or maple syrup to taste.

Ranch women are as sharp as nails and just as hard. If Eve had been a ranch-woman, she would never have tempted Adam with an apple. She would have ordered him to make his meal himself.

—Anthony Trollope, 1862

Cathead Biscuits with Chocolate Gravy

Demetra Bell-Runnels was a famous trick rider. Now she lives on a ranch outside Dallas, Texas, and can whip up real, old-timey breakfast biscuits, which she tops with an unbelievable gravy. She says, "I'm happy to share this with other Cowgirls, but I give all of the credit to my sweet mother, Brenda Bell. I love these with chocolate gravy, another family recipe. My husband, Mike, loves them cut open with any good pancake syrup poured over the top."

Serves 4

> 3 cups self-rising flour
> 1 rounded teaspoon baking powder
> ½ cup canola oil
> 1 cup buttermilk
> 1 cup low-fat milk
> 1 cup all-purpose flour

Preheat the oven to 450°F.

Grease a large cast-iron skillet. (You can use a large Pyrex pie plate, too.)

In a large mixing bowl, combine the self-rising flour and baking powder. Add the canola oil and use a fork to press it into the flour mixture until it looks "mealy."

Add the buttermilk and stir (the mixture should still look kind of dry), then add the low-fat milk and stir. The mixture should be wet and not really sticking to the bowl.

Pour 1 cup all-purpose flour on waxed paper. Using a big spoon, drop the dough one tablespoon at a time and roll in the flour. (I use my hands and not a biscuit cutter.)

Place the dough balls in the skillet, then top them with just a little oil in a teaspoon. Give them a little "love tap" with the bottom of a kitchen spoon.

Bake for about 30 minutes in the preheated oven. They will resemble cat's heads.

Chocolate Gravy

1½ cups sugar
⅓ cup cocoa (slightly less)
⅓ cup self-rising flour (slightly less)
1 (12-ounce) can evaporated milk
½ can water
2 tablespoons butter

Mix the dry ingredients in a saucepan. Add the evaporated milk, water, and butter.

Cook over medium heat, stirring constantly until the gravy thickens. If it starts to get too thick, add some milk.

The real things haven't changed. It is still best to be honest and truthful; to make the most of what we have; to be happy with simple pleasures; and to be cheerful and have courage when things go wrong.

—Laura Ingalls Wilder

Cinnamon Roll Pancakes

I am pretty sure you have a box of Bisquick in your pantry. I know I certainly do! Here's a recipe from our friends at Bisquick I'll bet you haven't tried.

Makes approximately 24 pancakes

> 2¼ cups Bisquick Complete, divided
> 1 cup milk, plus 1 tablespoon
> 2 eggs
> ¼ cup butter, melted
> ⅔ cup loosely packed brown sugar
> 3 tablespoons cinnamon
> 1 tablespoon vanilla
> Nonstick baking spray

In a large bowl, whisk together 2 cups Bisquick, 1 cup milk, and both of the eggs, until smooth. Set aside.

Preheat a griddle to medium heat.

In a small bowl, combine the melted butter, brown sugar, the remaining Bisquick and milk, cinnamon, and vanilla. Whisk together until smooth. Add a teaspoon more of milk if needed to make the cinnamon mixture thin enough for piping.

Transfer the cinnamon mixture into a large plastic bag. Snip a small corner from the bag.

Spray your hot griddle with nonstick baking spray. Transfer ⅓ cup of batter to the griddle. Immediately pipe a swirl of cinnamon around your pancake, so it looks like a cinnamon roll.

Spray a thin layer of nonstick baking spray right over the top of your pancake. When it's ready to flip, flip it and cook on the other side until golden brown.

Serve with your favorite maple syrup.

PHOTO COURTESY OF LYNETTE SMITH PHOTOGRAPHY

Handy Breakfast

This ingenious recipe came to me by way of a ranch wife living out in northern Idaho. She says, "With a toddler to feed, a husband to make breakfast for, and often as not, a puppy or a kitten to take care of in the kitchen, I find this lets me eat with one hand and tend to the rest with the other one."

Serves 8

> 16 slices bacon
> Nonstick cooking spray
> 1 (16.3-ounce) tube refrigerated buttermilk biscuits
> 8 eggs
> Salt and pepper to taste

Preheat the oven to 350°F.

In a 10-inch skillet, cook the bacon over medium heat about 4 minutes or until cooked but not crisp, turning once. (It will continue to cook in the oven.) Drain and set aside on a paper towel.

Spray 8 (6-ounce) muffin cups or 8 (6-ounce) glass custard cups with cooking spray. Separate the dough into 8 biscuits.

Place a biscuit in each muffin cup, pressing the dough three-fourths of the way up the sides of the cups. Place 2 bacon slices in each biscuit cup, and crack an egg over each. Season with salt and pepper.

Bake 25 to 30 minutes or until egg whites are set. Run a small knife around the cups to loosen. Serve immediately.

June's Eggs

A Cowgirl will always come to the rescue. When I lamented the fact that I had to serve a buffet-style brunch to a crowd and could not figure out what to do about the eggs, June Lee came to my rescue. This easy-to-make dish, one spiral-sliced ham, a dozen cinnamon rolls, and a bowl of fresh melon balls and I was all set!

Serves 8

> 10 eggs
> ½ cup all-purpose flour
> 1 teaspoon baking powder
> 2 cups small-curd cottage cheese
> 2 cups grated jack cheese
> ½ cup butter, melted
> 2 (4-ounce) cans green chiles, seeded and diced

Preheat the oven to 350°F.

Spray a 9 x 13-inch baking dish with cooking spray.

Beat the eggs. Fold in everything else, and pour the mixture into the prepared baking dish.

Bake for 35 minutes, until puffed up and browned slightly on top.

Napkin Bread

Napkin Bread, also called Sticky Bread, Golden Crown, Pinch-Me Bread, or Bubbleloaf, got its name from me because you need several napkins for your sticky fingers. Recipes for the bread first appeared in women's magazines and community cookbooks in the 1950s. Serve it hot so that the baked segments can be easily torn away with the fingers and eaten by hand.

Serves 4

> ½ cup granulated sugar
> 1 teaspoon cinnamon
> 1 (16.3-ounce) tube refrigerated buttermilk biscuits
> ½ cup chopped pecans (optional)
> ½ cup raisins (optional)
> ½ cup firmly packed brown sugar
> ½ cup butter or margarine, melted

Preheat the oven to 350°F.

Grease a 12-cup fluted tube pan (also known as a Bundt pan) with butter.

In a large plastic bag, mix together the granulated sugar and cinnamon.

Separate the dough into 8 biscuits, then cut each biscuit into quarters. Put them in the bag and shake to coat them thoroughly.

Arrange the biscuit pieces all around in the pan, adding walnuts and raisins (if using) among the pieces.

In a small bowl, mix the brown sugar and melted butter. Pour over the biscuit pieces.

Bake for 30 minutes or until golden brown and no longer doughy in the center.

Cool in the pan for 10 minutes, then turn upside down onto a serving plate. Pull apart to serve.

Frosting

Frosting is optional, but very good. Simply mix together:

  1 cup powdered sugar
  ¼ cup lemon juice
  Enough milk to thin the frosting to about ¼ cup

Using a fork, add the milk slowly until the frosting has no lumps and will "drizzle" easily.

Pass the napkins.

JILL CHARLOTTE STANFORD

All-American Steak 'N' Eggs

A truly hearty breakfast, but also remember that "breakfast for dinner" can be a wonderful way to end the day. Simple and easy.

Serves 4

> 1 tablespoon vegetable oil
> 1 1-pound sirloin, about 1 inch thick
> Sea salt and black pepper
> 2 tablespoons butter
> 8 large eggs

Preheat the oven to 350°F.

Preheat a large cast-iron skillet over medium heat until hot, about 5 minutes. Raise the heat to high and add the oil.

Season the steak generously with salt and pepper. Place the steak in the skillet and cook, turning once, until well-browned, about 4 minutes per side. Transfer the steak from the skillet to a platter. Place in the oven and cook for 5 minutes more for medium-rare.

Transfer the steak to a cutting board. Cover it loosely with foil and let it rest for 10 minutes before carving. Turn off the oven and put 4 plates in to warm.

While the steak is resting, cook the eggs. Heat 2 skillets over medium-low heat, a tablespoon of butter in each pan. Break 4 eggs into each skillet. Season the eggs lightly with salt and pepper, and cook until the whites are just set, about 3½ minutes. (If you want the yolks to be cooked through, cover and continue cooking for 1 to 2 minutes more.) Divide the eggs onto the 4 plates you've warmed in the oven.

The reason it is a good idea to let meats rest is so the juices can go back into the meat.

Cut the steak on a diagonal into thick slices, put them on the plates, and serve immediately. You might want some thick slices of buttered toast to sop up the egg yolks. Just sayin'...

Mabel Strickland, "Queen Mabel"

Born Mabel DeLong in 1897 near Walla Walla, Washington, Mabel was a natural horsewoman. Taking lessons from trick rider Bill Donovan, she won the trick riding contest in Walla Walla three years in a row (1913, 1914, and 1915) and quickly gained a reputation as an accomplished relay rider. (You can see her as a relay rider in the photo on page vi.) She joined a racing entourage and competed as a relay rider throughout the Northwest. She was a great trick rider, did some roping, and topped it off by riding broncs.

Mabel married bronc rider and calf roper Hugh Strickland in 1918. She was inducted in to the National Cowboy & Western Heritage Museum Hall of Fame, the ProRodeo Cowboys Hall of Fame, the National Cowgirl Hall of Fame, the Pendleton Hall of Fame, and the Cheyenne Frontier Days Hall of Fame. She died January 3, 1976, one of the last of the great "wild women."

My horse's feet are as swift as rolling thunder
He carries me away from all my fears
And when the world threatens to fall asunder
His mane is there to wipe away my tears.

—*Bonnie Lewis*

Breads

Cowgirls (and many Cowboys) never pass up a slice of good bread, a hot roll, or a fresh doughnut. Pass the butter, please. And jam while you're at it.

Baking Powder Butter Biscuits

"Roll out, cowboys!" Many a ranch hand has heard that call early in the morning. Baking powder biscuits (and gravy) are a staple in the cookhouse of ranches all over the West in the morning. Here is a one-pan, one-bowl recipe that will make you feel like going and branding something. Instead of gravy, serve with honey or jam. Or, what the hell, have the country gravy!

Makes 9 biscuits

> 1 stick (½ cup) butter
> 2½ cups all-purpose flour
> 4 teaspoons granulated sugar
> 4 teaspoons baking powder
> 2 teaspoons salt
> 1¾ cups buttermilk

Preheat the oven to 450°F.

In the baking dish that you'll be baking these biscuits in, melt the stick of butter in the microwave. Set aside.

In a medium bowl, mix together the flour, sugar, baking powder, and salt. Pour in the buttermilk and stir until a loose dough forms. The batter will be a bit sticky.

Using your hands, press the biscuit dough into the baking dish right on top of the melted butter. (If you use wet fingers, you won't stick to the dough as easily.) Some of the butter will run over the top of the dough—it will look like a mess, but don't worry.

Using a sharp knife, cut the biscuit dough into 9 squares or lines before putting the biscuits in the oven.

Bake for about 20 to 25 minutes, rotating the dish once during baking, until the biscuits are golden brown on top.

Remove from the oven and let cool before cutting all the way through. Use a spatula to remove the biscuits.

PHOTO BY ROBIN JOHNSON

Bear Signs Old-Fashioned Doughnuts

"The story behind this, as I was told, is when a cowboy goes courtin' a lady, she would make him these Bear Signs as a token she favored him. This is an old-fashioned cowboy recipe." My deepest thanks to "Mountain Woman" Caprice Madison for this.

Makes 2 dozen doughnuts

> 1 cup buttermilk
> 2 eggs, beaten
> 1 cup granulated sugar
> ⅓ cup butter or margarine, melted
> 2 tablespoons baking powder
> ½ teaspoon salt
> ½ teaspoon cinnamon
> 4 cups all-purpose flour
> Vegetable oil
> Powdered sugar

In the first bowl, mix the buttermilk, eggs, granulated sugar, and melted butter until well blended.

In a second bowl, combine the baking powder, salt, cinnamon, and flour.

Slowly add the dry ingredients to the first bowl, stirring them together. This mix should be stiff enough to hold a spoon upright; if not, mix in more flour. Knead together lightly for a minute or so, then turn out onto a floured board or countertop.

Use a rolling pin, an empty bottle, or the heels of your hands to roll the dough out to about one finger-width high (¼ inch). Cut circles out with a small glass, and set aside for about 5 minutes.

Meanwhile, pour 1 inch of oil into a large skillet and heat to 375°F. It's hot enough when a bread cube browns in about 1 minute.

Slide the dough circles into the frying pan and brown one side. Turn over and brown the other. Set out to drain on a plate covered with paper towels. Sprinkle with powdered sugar and eat warm.

Hold on to what is good even if it is a handful of earth. Hold on to what you believe even if it is a tree which stands by itself. Hold on to what you must do even if it is a long way from here. Hold on to life even when it is easier letting go. Hold on to my hand even when I have gone away from you.

—Nancy Wood, "Hold on to What Is Good"

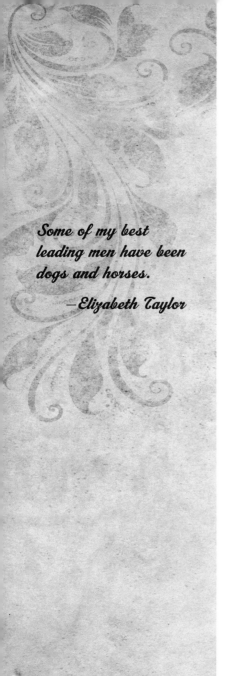

Cherokee Grape Dumplings

The Cherokee Nation calls these dumplings *tsalagi*. I call them very, very good! These came to me by way of an Irishman who was at the Cherokee Festival in North Carolina. Thanks, Michael!

Makes approximately 24 dumplings

>2 cups grape juice, plus ½ cup
>1 cup all-purpose flour
>1½ teaspoons baking powder
>2 teaspoons sugar
>¼ teaspoon salt
>1 tablespoon shortening

Heat 2 cups of grape juice in a saucepan to nearly boiling.

Mix the flour, baking powder, sugar, and salt. Add the shortening and cut it in, like for pie dough. Add ½ cup of grape juice and mix into a stiff dough.

Roll the dough very thin on a floured board and cut into strips ½ inch wide (or roll the dough in your hands and break off pea-size bits).

Drop the dumplings into the boiling grape juice and cook for 10 to12 minutes.

Use a slotted spoon to remove the dumplings from the hot juice. Serve warm with cream.

Miss Rodeo USA's Prize-Winning Banana Bread

Mackenzie Carr, Miss Rodeo USA 2012, is beautiful, rides like a champion, is always smiling, is always helpful, and is never anything but a true person. And, she cooks. Her mom, Barb Carr, says, "Mack makes a fabulous banana bread. It's a former Champion Bread from her 4-H days at the Columbia County [Oregon] Fair." I certainly give it a Blue Ribbon!

Makes 2 loaves

> ½ cup shortening
> 2 cups sugar
> 2 eggs, slightly beaten
> ¼ teaspoon salt
> 1½ teaspoons baking soda
> 3 "old" bananas, mashed
> 3 cups all-purpose flour
> 10 tablespoons buttermilk
> 1 teaspoon vanilla
> 1 tablespoon dark molasses

Preheat the oven to 350°F.

Grease two 3½ x 4½ x 2½-inch loaf pans.

Cream the shortening and the sugar until fluffy. Add the eggs, salt, and baking soda and blend well.

Add the bananas and flour, alternating one banana with one cup of flour. Mix thoroughly.

Add the buttermilk, vanilla, and molasses and mix again.

Pour the batter into the loaf pans. Bake for 1 hour or until the center is done.

Let the loaves cool, then turn out of the pans.

JILL CHARLOTTE STANFORD

Marti's Yeast Rolls

Makes approximately 2 dozen rolls

When I spoke with Marti Lee, a Cowgirl who lives in Senatobia, Mississippi, about my failure at making *anything at all* with yeast, she assured me she had a fail-safe recipe. I said if her recipe worked for me, then anyone could do it, so could I have the recipe, please? She sent it in this form, and by golly, it's like having her stand next to you (me) in the kitchen. And guess what? It worked! So listen up while she talks you through it.

   1 packet (2 teaspoons) rapid-rise yeast
   ½ cup warm water (warm but not hot—that will kill the yeast)
   4 tablespoons sugar, divided
   1 stick (½ cup) butter
   2 cups buttermilk
   5 cups all-purpose flour
   1 teaspoon salt
   1 teaspoon baking soda

Add the yeast to the warm water along with 2 tablespoons of sugar to get things going. Let this set somewhere away from cold drafts while you are gathering and prepping the other ingredients.

Put the butter and buttermilk in a microwave-safe bowl and melt them in the microwave for about 1 minute. The buttermilk will separate and that is okay. Set it aside.

Place the flour in a large bowl. Add to it the salt, 2 more tablespoons of sugar, and the baking soda and stir to mix.

Add the yeast to the flour mixture, along with the butter and buttermilk. Mix well till it makes a stiff dough, adding more flour if need be, but this is usually enough.

Place the dough in a well-greased bowl, cover with plastic wrap, and let rise till doubled, about 45 minutes to 1 hour.

Punch the dough down and shape into whatever kind of rolls your want— usually I just make 'em into balls the size of a ping-pong ball in a large, well-greased baking pan.

Let them rise again till doubled and then bake in a 350°F oven for about 20 minutes until the tops are golden brown.

Remove from the oven and brush the tops with melted butter.

Try to let 'em cool a few minutes before you dig in! I hope y'all enjoy 'em as much as we do! They are big, dense, and soul warming!

When playing hard to get,
it's better to have a fast horse.

—Anonymous

Summer Bread

No one says "no" to chocolate. Here is the perfect answer to an overabundance of zucchini from your garden, or a well-meaning friend's garden. Some Cowgirls frost this with a simple chocolate frosting and serve it as a dessert with ice cream. I like to put cream cheese on a warm slice and serve it for lunch with a simple green salad.

Makes 2 loaves

   3 eggs
   2 cups sugar
   ½ cup vegetable oil
   ½ cup applesauce
   3 teaspoons vanilla
   ½ cup whole milk
   2 cups shredded zucchini
   1 teaspoon salt
   1 teaspoon baking soda
   ½ teaspoon baking powder
   ½ cup cocoa
   2½ cups all-purpose flour

Preheat the oven to 375°F.

In a large bowl, beat the eggs and add the sugar. Beat again. Add the oil, applesauce, vanilla, and milk. Stir well, then add the zucchini.

Sift together the salt, baking soda, baking powder, cocoa, and flour. Add this gradually to the wet ingredients.

Pour into 2 greased 3½ x 4½ x 2½-inch loaf pans. Bake for 55 minutes. Check with a toothpick for doneness—the tops should be a little bit "cracked." Let the loaves cool before turning out on a wire rack. Like chocolate chip cookies, this is best eaten a little warm.

Hazel Walker

Hazel Agnes Wedderien Walker (aka Peggy Warren) was born in 1889. She traveled the early rodeo circuit in the twentieth-century teens and was married to a cowboy named Frank Walker. Hazel competed in bronco busting, trick riding, relay races, and the pony race. She rodeoed at the Pendleton Round-Up in 1912, 1913, and 1916; the Calgary Stampede in 1912; the Winnipeg Stampede in 1913; and the Los Angeles Rodeo in 1912 and 1913. Her second husband was a Mr. Warren, and from then on she was known as, and competed as, Peggy Warren.

GLENBOW ARCHIVES #NA-335-25

Appetizers, Salads, and Sides

It's the trimmings that make a meal memorable. An appetizer before a meal, a good salad, or something from the garden make your taste buds stand up and say "Wha hoo!"

GLENBOW ARCHIVES #NA 4727-4

Patty's Shrimp

True story. When I was a guest at a working cattle ranch in eastern Oregon, I offered to help out in the kitchen. I thought something to eat before dinner would be nice while the cowboys had a beer or ice tea. I had noticed "Cookie" had a bottle of vermouth (it was pretty dusty) in the pantry, and I knew just what to fix. After heading off to the store (which was 30 miles away) for most of the ingredients and back, I prepared an appetizer for the evening meal. The cowboys were not too sure about it until they had some. They liked it. I got a postcard from Cookie a week or so later, asking for the recipe for "Patty's Shrimp." He said, "The boys have been asking for it again."

So I wrote out the recipe for Shrimp Pâté and sent it back to the Rural Route. I expect they are still enjoying it.

Serves 6 appreciative ranch hands

1 pound cooked shrimp meat
1 pound cream cheese
½ teaspoon dill weed
1 teaspoon Dijon mustard
3 green onions, finely chopped
2 tablespoons chopped parsley
1 teaspoon lemon juice
Dash of dry vermouth or to taste

Chop up the shrimp a little, then combine all the other ingredients well.

Put the mixture into the bowl it will be served in, and refrigerate until you are ready to serve it with crackers. PS: I did not get fancy on the boys—I bought Ritz.

PHOTO BY ROBIN JOHNSON

Cowgirl's Caviar

Quite a few Cowgirls asked if this recipe, known as Cowboy Caviar, was going to be in the new book. "Well, of course," I said. "And I am renaming it, too." This was met with general approval.

Serves 4

    4 cups peeled and diced tomatoes
    1 medium sweet onion, diced
    1 green bell pepper, seeded and diced
    1 (16-ounce) bag frozen corn, thawed and drained
    1 (16-ounce) can black-eyed peas, drained
    1½ cups Italian dressing
    1 tablespoon chopped cilantro
    Sour cream

Combine all the ingredients well. I recommend a blender on low and not for very long. Put this into an attractive bowl and garnish with a dollop (or two) of sour cream.

Serve with tortilla chips and your favorite drink, and put your feet up and enjoy the sunset.

If you're lucky enough to be a cowgirl, you're lucky enough.

—Anonymous

Goin' to Heaven Ambrosia

You can call this corny—it is. You can call this old-fashioned—it is. This is the "perfect" salad side dish to take to a potluck or to serve at the table. Men love it, and Cowgirls think it is heaven on a plate. Corny, but heaven nevertheless. I had this in a small Western town, in the Grange Hall, at a potluck and thought it was danged good. Thanks to Luella Parsons for sharing!

Serves 6

    1 (8-ounce) can mandarin oranges, drained
    1 (8-ounce) can pineapple chunks, drained
    1 cup miniature marshmallows
    1 cup flaked coconut
    1 cup (8 ounces) sour cream or ready-made whipped cream (This is entirely up
    to you. A combination, half and half, is good, too.)
    ½ cup chopped walnuts or pecans (optional)

Mix all the ingredients together well, and refrigerate until well chilled.

Some people garnish this with maraschino cherries, which I think is an awfully good idea.

> *She never shook the stars from their*
> *appointed courses. But she loved good*
> *men. And she rode good horses.*
>
> *—Margot Liberty*

Trick Riders' Orange and Cranberry Sauce

Peggy Veach-Robinson is the daughter of Monroe Veach, maker of the best trick-riding saddles. Peggy herself was a trick rider in her younger days. Today, she runs the saddle shop in Trenton, Missouri, where they not only make trick saddles, but all kinds and styles of Western saddles. Here is a neat "trick" from Peggy for your next Thanksgiving.

Serves 6–8

> 1 (11-ounce) can mandarin oranges
> 1 (12-ounce) package fresh or frozen cranberries
> ¾ cup sugar
> 1 teaspoon ground ginger
> ½ cup chopped pecans

Drain the oranges, but reserve ¼ cup of the syrup.

In a medium-size microwave-safe bowl, microwave the cranberries, sugar, and ginger in the reserved orange syrup on high for 7 to 11 minutes, or until the cranberries pop.

Stir in the oranges and nuts.

Chill and serve.

Oven-Baked Hard-Boiled Eggs

Preheat the oven to 350°F. Put the eggs on the lower rack and bake for 30 minutes. (You can put them in the cups of a muffin tin if you're afraid they will roll off the rack.) Prepare a bowl of ice water. Use tongs and put the baked eggs in the water for 10 minutes. This stops the eggs from cooking.

I think this is an amazing tip, don't you? This method makes them easier to peel. And, they don't break in the boiling water, making them useless for hard-boiled egg recipes.

Cowgirl Slaw

Not your mother's coleslaw, that's for sure! This one packs a punch as well as a kick.

Serves 8

> 1 small head green cabbage, finely shredded
> 1 orange, juiced
> 1 lime, juiced
> 1 teaspoon salt
> 1 teaspoon sugar
> 1 tablespoon tequila
> 1 tomato, finely diced
> 2 tablespoons finely diced jalapeño (optional)
> 1 tablespoon olive oil

Put the shredded cabbage in a glass bowl.

Mix the orange juice, lime juice, salt, sugar, and tequila together in a separate bowl. Let stand for a few minutes so the sugar can dissolve.

Pour the juice mixture over the cabbage, tossing to combine. Stir in the tomato, optional jalapeño, and olive oil and mix the slaw lightly.

Cover and let stand in the refrigerator for 30 minutes before serving.

A Few of My Favorite Things Deviled Eggs

My list of favorite things is very long. Right up there in the top 10 is bacon! A few spots below that is cheese; namely, cheddar cheese. Well, any cheese, but cheddar is comfort food for me. When I was a small girl, I made mayonnaise sandwiches. No meat . . . just mayo. Eggs? Not so much, except for deviled eggs. I have always loved them. So, I put all these together and here they are!

Serves 12 (because you will take 2)

> 4 slices bacon
> 12 hard-boiled eggs, peeled and cut in half lengthwise
> ½ cup mayonnaise
> 2 tablespoons shredded cheddar cheese
> 1 teaspoon yellow mustard

Fry the bacon until crisp. Drain on paper towels and crumble.

Remove the egg yolks and put them in a small bowl. Mash them using a fork. Then add the mayonnaise, the crumbled bacon, and the cheese. Stir the mustard in last.

Fill the egg-white halves with the yolk mixture. Be sure to keep them in the refrigerator until ready to serve.

You could, and I have, use blue cheese, crumbled, instead of cheddar in this recipe. Or, and I have done this too, use ranch dressing instead of mayonnaise and mustard.

Garden Zucchini Fritters

Anyone who has ever grown a garden anywhere in the United States has made the mistake of planting one too many zucchini. This leads to the old jokes about people in small towns locking their cars during the height of summer to keep from coming back and finding a backseat full of zucchini. Or finding a large zucchini in your mailbox, unwanted and unasked for. Well! Try this recipe and you'll be going door-to-door asking, "Any spare zucchini?"

Serves 4

> 1 pound zucchini, or 1 large zucchini
> Salt
> 1 green onion, chopped (stems, or green part, only)
> ½ teaspoon minced jalapeño
> 1 teaspoon cumin seed
> 2 tablespoons all-purpose flour
> 1 egg, beaten
> ¼ cup olive oil
> Greek-style yogurt for garnish

Shred the zucchini and put it in a colander. Sprinkle generously with salt and mix well, then put it aside, in the sink, to drain.

Rinse the shredded zucchini under cold water. Pick up a small handful and squeeze it dry, then put that handful in a clean kitchen towel. When you have squeezed all the zucchini, gather up the towel and twist it to wring out any excess liquid.

Put the zucchini in a bowl and add the green onion, jalapeño, and cumin. Stir in the flour, and then the beaten egg. The mix will be sticky. If there is still some liquid, add a little more flour.

Pour the olive oil into a nonstick skillet. Heat the oil until it is hot enough to make a piece of zucchini sizzle.

Drop 4 mounds of the zucchini mixture (2 to 3 tablespoons) into the pan, flattening them a little with the back of the spoon. Fry until golden brown, about 3 to 4 minutes. Flip over and fry for 2 to 3 minutes more.

Remove to a paper towel and pat away excess oil. Serve immediately with a dollop (heaping tablespoon) of thick Greek yogurt.

Cowgirl Texting

Modern-day Cowgirls have cell phones. They have their own form of texting, too.

FYI: For y'alls information
WTF: What to fry
BYOB: Bring your own biscuits
HYH: Hold your horses
OMG: Order more grits
DTBA: Don't that beat all
OTD: Older than dirt
CU: Cowgirl up!
BYH: Bless your heart

You can save the scooped-out potato and make mashed potatoes or potato pancakes for breakfast!

Chorizo is made from coarsely chopped pork and pork fat, seasoned with smoked paprika and salt. It is generally classed as either picante *(spicy) or* dulce *(sweet), depending upon the type of smoked paprika used. It is available in nearly every grocery store.*

Hot and Spicy Potato Skins

Many of you who have read my book *Wild Women and Tricky Ladies* will be familiar with Jan Mendoza. She qualifies as a Cowgirl for more reasons than I can list here. Here is something she likes to serve. It is also a guaranteed big hit for a potluck.

Serves 24 for a party tray or 12 as a side dish

> 12 red russet potatoes
> 1 pound spicy chorizo
> 1 cup grated sharp cheddar cheese
> ½ cup sour cream

Microwave or bake the potatoes until done.

While the potatoes are cooking, cook the chorizo in a skillet until there is no pinkness.

Cut the cooked potatoes in half and scoop out the centers (leave just a little potato so that the skin is thick). Fill the potatoes with the cooked chorizo and top with the cheddar cheese.

Place the potato halves on a cookie sheet and put them under the broiler until the cheese is slightly melted.

Top with a dab of sour cream and serve them hot!

Suzi's Southwestern Rice

"Get a move on!" is Suzi Hazard's favorite saying. She is up at the crack of dawn and on one of the many horses she trains for clients all over the Southwest. In addition to giving clinics, she likes to cook, but "nuthin' too hard or too special," she says. This fills the bill. "It's even better the next day and, besides, you don't have to cook it the next day," Suzi adds with a twinkle in her eye.

Serves 6 hungry riders

> 1 (14½-ounce) can stewed tomatoes, undrained
> 1 (15½-ounce) can black beans, rinsed and drained
> 1 cup instant brown rice
> 1 cup canned corn (or fresh, scraped off the cob)
> 1 tablespoon cumin
> ½ teaspoon chili powder
> Salt and pepper to taste

Put everything in a large pan or skillet with a lid that fits tightly.

Bring to a boil, reduce the heat, and simmer for about 10 minutes or until the liquid is absorbed.

Add salt and pepper to taste.

The Salad

In my family, that is the only title or description needed. We all know, instantly, what it is. We have made this every year for Christmas or Thanksgiving dinner since 1969. Now you can, too!

Serves 6

1 (14-ounce) can whole-berry cranberry sauce
3 tablespoons lemon juice
1 cup heavy cream, whipped (If you are pressed for time—and who isn't these days?—you can substitute ready-made whipped cream.)
1 cup broken walnut and pecan meats
¼ cup mayonnaise
¼ cup powdered sugar

JILL CHARLOTTE STANFORD

Mix the cranberry sauce and lemon juice together (be careful not to "bruise" the cranberries) and spread it in a 6 x 6-inch Pyrex dish.

Mix the whipped cream, nuts, mayonnaise, and sugar together and spread it on top of the cranberry mixture.

Freeze for at least 3 hours.

To serve, let it thaw for about 10 minutes, cut into squares, and serve on lettuce leaves. A dollop of mayonnaise is the big finish.

The RRR

A very simple and surprisingly good salad. The peppery radishes, the crisp romaine, the subtle ranch ... heaven.

Serves 4

> 1 head romaine lettuce, dark outer leaves taken off, chopped
> 8–10 large radishes, tops and bottoms taken off, diced
> Ranch dressing

Put the chopped lettuce and radishes in a bowl. Pour on as much ranch dressing as you want, mix, and serve.

You know you are a Cowgirl if . . . the "wanna-be-a-professional" work car has dust and kitty prints all over the outside and hay stems covering the floor board. The once lovely interior smells of molasses and grain from using the car at lunch to buy grain for your horses.

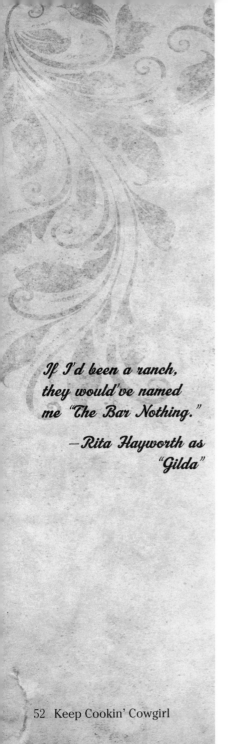

Back at the Ranch Dressing

I'll admit it, I love ranch dressing. Why? Because there are so many good things you can do with it: on salad greens, poured over a baked potato, and for dipping crisp veggies and BBQ chicken wings in. I like to make my own, and I like to make it simple and basic.

Makes 1½ cups

> 1 cup good buttermilk
> ¼ cup mayonnaise
> 3 tablespoons sour cream
> 2 teaspoons lemon juice
> 1 medium garlic clove, finely chopped
> ½ teaspoon sea salt
> ⅛ teaspoon freshly ground black pepper

Put all the ingredients in a 16-ounce Mason jar. Close it tight and shake as hard as you can to mix the ingredients. Taste and season with additional salt and pepper as desired.

Refrigerate until chilled and the flavors have melded, about 1 hour. The dressing will last up to 3 days in the refrigerator. You can pour it right from the jar—no need for a fancy salad dressing boat.

If I'd been a ranch, they would've named me "The Bar Nothing."

—Rita Hayworth as "Gilda"

Lily's Salad Dressing

I met Lily at a horse auction. We struck up a conversation while eyeing a dapple gray mare neither one of us could afford. I learned that Lily had been a sheepherder in her early years and then settled on a small ranch in central Oregon, where she raised a few fine horses for "everyday work," as she put it. She invited me for lunch and more reminiscing of her days out on the prairies all by herself. Her salad dressing was like nothing I've ever tasted, and she was pouring it out of a Mason jar, over a wedge of iceberg lettuce. I persuaded her to share the recipe.

Makes 3 cups

> 1 (10.75-ounce) can tomato soup, undiluted
> ½ soup can of vegetable oil
> ½ soup can of white vinegar
> Salt, pepper, and sugar to taste

Put all the ingredients in a quart jar, cover, and shake well. You can add onion (peeled and chopped), 2 tablespoons of dry mustard, or crumbled blue cheese if you want to get really fancy. Keeps well for weeks in the refrigerator.

It is a disease for which there is no cure. You will go on riding even after they have to haul you on a comfortable, wise old cob, with feet like inverted buckets and a back like a fireside chair.

—Monica Dickens

Goldie St. Clair

Goldie St. Clair was a performer with Miller Brothers 101 Ranch and won both the 1909 and 1910 Women's Bronco Riding Contest. She always rode the broncs brandishing a quirt. In the 1910 contest, former president Theodore Roosevelt expressed concern that she might be hurt. The following year, in Philadelphia, a bronc named Roan Mare fell on her, causing life-threatening injuries. Here is the newspaper account:

> *April 20, 1911, Philadelphia—In a battle between a girl and an outlaw horse, which has a record as a man killer, Miss Goldie St. Clair probably fulfilled Colonel Roosevelt's recent prediction that a "bad horse would finally get her." The young woman was crushed beneath the bronco after a struggle in the arena of the 101 Ranch Show yesterday afternoon.*
>
> *Miss St. Clair, who won the ex-president's praise last August at Cheyenne, Wyoming, in the Frontier Days contests, when she retained her title as champion "woman bronco buster," is near death today. The accident appalled hundreds who were seated about the arena at the conclusion of a performance of thrilling feats of horsemanship. Miss St. Clair undertook to ride Roan Mare, known throughout the west as the worst type of man killing outlaw horse. The animal fell on Miss St. Clair, crushing the pommel of the saddle against her head.*

You can't keep a good cowgirl down, and Goldie St. Clair was back performing and riding broncs a few months later.

Soups and Stews

Nothing is more satisfying to a tired and cold Cowgirl than a bowl of savory stew or soup at the end of a long day gathering and branding. This is where that slow cooker can come in handy!

Back at the Bunkhouse Chili

"This is guaranteed to make your crew happy after the branding," say Terry Wilcox. She ought to know. They run a big herd in Colorado, and there is a lot of branding to be done.

Serves 8

> 5 strips bacon
> 2 pounds ground beef
> 1 onion, peeled and chopped
> 4 ripe tomatoes, peeled and chopped
> 2 cloves garlic, peeled and chopped
> 2 tablespoons chili powder
> 1 (16-ounce) can tomato sauce
> 3 (1-pound) cans red kidney beans
> Salt and pepper to taste

In a skillet, fry the bacon until it is crisp. Drain on a paper towel. When it is cool, cut it into pieces.

Add the ground beef into the skillet. Stir and cook until it is well done.

Add the onion, tomatoes, garlic, chili powder, tomato sauce, and beans. Cover and simmer for at least 1 hour.

Add salt and pepper to your taste. If it's really cold outside, add a dash of green Tabasco sauce.

Terry sometimes mixes everything in a Crock-Pot and just lets it go on the low setting for the day.

Chilly Roasted Tomato Soup

good!

On a warm summer's evening after a hot day out on the range, nothing tastes better than a chilled soup with a gourmet flavor. This is best made the day before, if possible, and then kept in the refrigerator. The flavors deepen.

Serves 2–4

> 1½ tablespoons olive oil
> 3 pounds Roma tomatoes, halved
> 3 cloves garlic, peeled and halved
> 2 cups chicken broth
> ¼ cup chopped fresh basil, or 2 tablespoons dried
> 2 tablespoons fresh chopped rosemary, or 1 tablespoon dried
> ½ tablespoon balsamic vinegar
> Salt and pepper to taste
> Sour cream for garnish

Preheat the oven to 375°F.

Put the olive oil in an 8 x 10-inch baking dish and spread evenly. Toss in the tomatoes and the garlic, and stir them to coat them with the oil. Roast for about 1 hour. Be careful the tomatoes do not char.

Remove the roasted tomatoes and garlic from the oven and place in a food processor or blender. Add the chicken broth, basil, rosemary, and balsamic vinegar. Blend until smooth—then taste it. Adjust the seasonings by adding salt and pepper to your taste.

Cool the soup down and refrigerate until you are hungry. Divide it up into 2 large bowls or 4 smaller bowls. A dollop of sour cream on top and a loaf of bread with softened butter, and supper is ready!

Chuck Wagon Stew

This recipe comes from the days when the chuck wagon went out with the crew for branding and/or gathering the cattle. Those camp cooks had to be versatile and use whatever they had. The beef was fresh, of course, but they also took along some preserved pork as well as lamb (usually mutton, or "quite-a-bit-older lamb"). I have taken some liberties with the original recipe because, while it was filling and proved quite a bit of protein, it was, well, boring. Don't tell the camp cook, okay?

Serves 4

1 pound beef stew meat, cut into cubes
1 pound lamb, cut into cubes
1 pound pork, cut into cubes
¼ cup bacon fat or shortening
4 russet potatoes, peeled and diced
4 white onions, peeled and diced
1 16-ounce package frozen peas (or use fresh ones if you have a garden, about 2 cups)
1 (15.25-ounce) can corn (or 2 cups fresh and cut off the cob)
4 tomatoes, peeled and diced
2 cups water
¼ cup soy sauce (Don't weaken on this ingredient—it works!)
Salt and pepper
2 cups Burgundy wine

In a Dutch oven or Crock-Pot, brown the meat (which has been lightly dusted with flour) in the fat. I prefer bacon fat for the flavor, but you can use shortening.

Add the vegetables, water, soy sauce, and salt and pepper. Simmer, covered, over low heat for 5 hours or until the meats are very tender.

Add the wine. (See? Not boring any longer!) Simmer for 1 more hour with the lid off to allow the wine to evaporate. Add more salt and pepper to taste.

AUTHOR'S COLLECTION

Hearty Vegetable Soup

Robin Johnson is my sister, and she asked how she could help with the book. I asked for a really good vegetable soup, and here it is! She says, "Through the years I have fooled around with this recipe, and it comes out differently each time because it all depends on what is in the fridge and what I have on hand. Have fun with it. It's quick and easy and really better on the second day."

Serves 8 with plenty left over

> 2 tablespoons olive oil
> 1 cup diced yellow onion
> 1 cup diced carrots
> 1 cup diced celery
> 1 cup diced zucchini
> 1½ teaspoons oregano and/or basil
> 1 (14.5-ounce) can vegetable or chicken stock
> 1 cup shredded cabbage (cut into ½-inch strips)
> 1 (14.5-ounce) can diced tomatoes with juice
> 1 (14.5-ounce) can kidney beans, drained and rinsed
> 1 (14.5-ounce) can green beans, drained
> 5–7 drops hot sauce or to taste
> 1 teaspoon salt
> ⅛ teaspoon pepper

Heat the olive oil in a large soup pot and add the onion, carrots, and celery. Cook on medium-low heat for about 10 minutes, until the onion is translucent.

Add the zucchini and herbs and continue to sauté for a few minutes. Add the stock and bring to a boil, then reduce to a simmer for another 10 minutes or until the zucchini is cooked.

Add the cabbage and cook for a few minutes, then add the tomatoes and both beans. Bring the soup back up to temperature—but don't let it boil. Add the remaining seasonings carefully, tasting until you like what you've got!

Serve with grated Parmesan or other cheese if desired.

PHOTO BY ROBIN JOHNSON

If you want, at the end of the process, you can add some cut-up cooked chicken or turkey to this soup. Sliced gourmet-style sausage is good, too. Leftover pot roast is also a good choice—just use beef stock in place of the chicken stock. This is a thick soup with more vegetables than liquid. If you want it to be more soupy, add more stock. You can also add some cooked egg noodles, penne pasta, or rice—even diced potato (either white or sweet) added at the same time as the zucchini to make it even heartier!

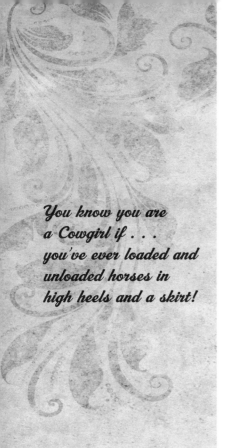

Irish Cowgirls' Stew

Many of the early day cowboys and cowgirls came from Irish stock. Their mams and paps had come from Ireland, seeking a new life in the West. They brought their treasured recipes with them, too. Here is one of them.

Serves 4

2 tablespoons vegetable oil

3½ pounds chuck roast, cut into 1-inch cubes

¼ cup all-purpose flour

Salt and pepper

12 ounces tomato paste

4 large carrots, cut into 1-inch-long chunks

1 large onion or 2 smaller ones, cut into 1-inch pieces

2½ pounds red potatoes, halved

10 cloves garlic, sliced

15 ounces Guinness Extra Stout Beer

2½ cups beef broth

1 (16-ounce) bag frozen peas

Preheat the oven to 350°F.

In a large oven-safe pot or Dutch oven, heat the oil over medium-high heat. Toss the beef cubes in flour to coat and season with salt and pepper.

Toss the beef with the hot oil and allow the beef to sear and brown for about 4 minutes. Stir and sear for another 3 to 4 minutes, or until the beef is a nice, deep brown color.

Reduce heat to medium and stir in the tomato paste. Add the carrots, onions, potatoes, garlic, beer, and broth. Season with more salt and pepper and bring to a boil.

Put the lid on the pot and place it in the oven. Cook for 2½ to 3 hours, or until meat is nice and tender.

Once you remove the pot from the oven, add the peas and stir. If your stew looks a little too thick, you can add ½ to 1 cup of water. Too thin? Mix a little flour or cornstarch in ½ cup of cold water, and add this to the hot gravy in the pot. Heat, stirring, until it thickens.

To be a cowgirl is more than just fluff and stuff. You have to do your share of the work, kill your own snakes, never complain, mount up even when you know you may get bucked off, and all the while being more of a lady at work than when you are at home.

—Georgie Sicking, National Cowgirl Hall of Fame honoree, 1989

Mom's Corn Chowder

Blair Woodfield, co-owner of the famed Hamley Steakhouse in Pendleton, Oregon, has shared this recipe of his mother's, which is served in the restaurant at least once a week. Born and raised in eastern Idaho, Wanda Ball Woodfield excelled in real ranch cooking. Growing up on the family sheep ranch and later married to a cattle rancher, she seamlessly incorporated both influences into a cooking style that pleased all who graced her table. Nobody left her table hungry or without an appreciation for food well prepared with sincere love and a warm heart. Enjoy Wanda's legendary corn chowder, an authentic dish from the ranch.

Serves 4

12 slices bacon, diced
2 chicken breasts, cut into ¼-inch cubes
1 onion, chopped
3 stalks celery, chopped
1½ cups chicken broth, divided
1½ cups whole-kernel corn, divided
4 white potatoes, peeled and diced
2 cups heavy cream
1 cup chopped fresh parsley
1 teaspoon salt
½ teaspoon white pepper

In a soup pot, cook the bacon until it is crisp, then remove it with a slotted spoon to a paper towel. Pour off all but 2 tablespoons of bacon drippings.

Add the chicken, onions, and celery to the pot and cook for 10 to 15 minutes, stirring frequently.

In a blender, combine ½ of the chicken broth and ½ of the corn. Blend on high speed until smooth.

Stir the pureed corn into the pot along with the remaining corn kernels, the potatoes, and the rest of the chicken broth. Bring to a boil over high heat, then reduce the heat to low and simmer for 20 minutes, partially covered, until the potatoes are tender.

Stir in the cream, parsley, salt, and pepper and simmer for another 2 to 3 minutes.

Finally, stir in the bacon. Adjust the salt and pepper to taste.

Always dress like you're going to see your worst enemy.

—Kimora Lee Simmons

Thick as Pea Soup

Many of my ancestors were Scots, so that explains why I am "thrifty"—some would say "cheap." Prowling the aisles at our local Bi-Mart, I spotted a six-pack of canned green peas for less than $3. My ancestors would be proud of me, but that's a lot of canned peas. Here is what I did with one can. The rest I'm not so sure about. Perhaps more soup?

JILL CHARLOTTE STANFORD

Serves 4

    1 (15-ounce) can peas
    2 tablespoons chopped onion
    ¼ cup butter
    ¼ cup all-purpose flour
    1 teaspoon sugar
    ½ teaspoon salt
    ⅛ teaspoon pepper
    ⅛ teaspoon rubbed sage
    2 cups water
    1 (12-ounce) can evaporated milk, or 1 cup half-and-half
    4 strips bacon, cooked and crumbled, or leftover ham pieces for garnish

Drain the peas but reserve ⅓ cup of the liquid. Place the peas and the reserved liquid in a blender or food processor; cover and puree until smooth. Set aside.

In a saucepan, sauté the onion in the butter until tender. Stir in the flour, sugar, salt, pepper, and sage and mix until smooth.

Gradually add the water and keep stirring until your mixture is thick and bubbly. Boil, stirring constantly, for 2 minutes.

Stir in the evaporated milk or half-and-half and the pureed peas. Cook, stirring occasionally, until the soup is hot.

Garnish with the bacon or ham.

Fish Chowder

While it is true that Cowgirls eat a lot of beef, they also like other dishes. I, personally, like a good, rich, hearty fish chowder now and then. Furthermore, it has bacon in it, another great favorite of mine.

Serves 6

4 slices bacon, chopped
1 large carrot, peeled and chopped
2 stalks celery, peeled and chopped
1 large white potato, peeled and chopped
2 tablespoons water, plus ½ cup
2 small white onions, chopped
2 tablespoons all-purpose flour
1 (8-ounce) can clams, drained with liquid reserved
1 cup bottled clam juice
1 pound whitefish (such as cod, sole, or catfish), cut into 1-inch chunks (You can also add a can of drained shrimp and/or crabmeat.)
½ cup milk
½ teaspoon sea salt
½ teaspoon freshly ground pepper
6 slices of toasted French bread

In a large saucepan, cook the bacon on medium heat until browned and crisp, turning occasionally. Drain on paper towels and set aside. Discard all but 1 tablespoon of the bacon fat.

While the bacon cooks, in a large microwave-safe bowl, combine the carrot, celery, potato, and 2 tablespoons water. Cover with vented plastic wrap and microwave on high for 5 minutes or until vegetables are just tender.

Keep the saucepan with the bacon fat on medium. Add the onions and cook 6 to 8 minutes or until tender, stirring occasionally. Add the vegetables and cook for 2 minutes, stirring.

Add the flour and cook 2 minutes more, stirring. Add the clam juice, reserved clam juice, and ½ cup water and whisk until smooth. Heat to boiling, stirring occasionally.

Add the fish chunks, cover, and cook 4 to 5 minutes or until the fish turns opaque throughout. Don't overcook the fish! Now stir in the milk, salt, and pepper. Add the drained clams (they get tough if cooked too long). Cook 1 to 2 minutes or until hot but not boiling. Crumble the cooled bacon.

Spoon the stew into shallow bowls that have a slice of toasted French bread in the bottom. Sprinkle the bacon on top.

Never dull your shine for somebody else.

—*Tyra Banks*

Flores LaDue

Flores LaDue was the stage name of Grace Bensell. She married Guy Weadick. Both were accomplished and talented trick ropers, working the vaudeville circuit and performing stunts in Western acts throughout North America and Europe. In 1912 they established one of the greatest outdoor shows on earth, the Calgary Exhibition & Stampede. Flores was known as "The First Lady of the Stampede." They eventually settled together in western Canada, and their final resting places are in the Foothills/ High River area. They were a loving couple to the end.

GLENBOW ARCHIVES #NA-446-106

Sheepherders' Lamb Shank Stew

My very first cookbook was *Lamb Country Cooking*. I am a big fan of lamb. I know that there were terrible conflicts between the sheepherders and the cattlemen in the early days, but no matter what you were trailing, you still had to stop and eat. Try this soup/stew dish with some crusty bread.

Serves 4

> 6 cups water or organic chicken broth
> 1 cup dry split peas, green or yellow
> 4 lamb shanks (no need to braise or brown first)
> 1 teaspoon thyme or rosemary
> 1 large garlic clove, sliced
> 1 teaspoon salt
> 6 crushed peppercorns
> 1 tablespoon rice, brown or white
> 2 large carrots, peeled and cut into rounds
> 1 large onion, coarsely chopped

Mix all the ingredients in a Crock-Pot or a heavy ovenproof casserole with a lid.

Bake in a preheated 300°F oven if using a casserole, or at the high setting if using a Crock-Pot, for 3 to 4 hours. Add more water if it gets too thick.

The shanks are perfect when they are tender when pricked with a fork and nearly falling off the bone.

Main Dishes

Gathered around the dinner table with friends in the ranch house is a Cowgirl's chance to catch up on the local gossip, what the price of hay is, and who got bucked off a green colt.

DENVER PUBLIC LIBRARY—WESTERN HISTORY DEPARTMENT #Z-689

Chicken Tortilla Casserole

Lindsey Martinez is a Cowgirl of the first degree in my eyes. She drives an eighteen-wheel flatbed truck, water-skis like a demon, befriends pit bulls that have been abused or neglected and finds good homes for them, and answered my question of "Do you want to contribute anything for this book?" by e-mailing me five minutes later. Did I mention she is beautiful to boot?

Serves 4

> 4 chicken breasts, cooked
> 1 (10-ounce) can cream of chicken soup
> 1 (7-ounce) can green chile salsa
> 2 tablespoons quick-cooking tapioca
> 6–8 corn tortillas, torn into pieces
> Shredded cheddar cheese, about 2 cups worth

Cut or shred the chicken into bite-size pieces and mix well with the soup, salsa, and tapioca.

Lightly grease the bottom of a Crock-Pot and then add ⅓ of the tortilla pieces.

Add ⅓ of chicken and soup mixture and sprinkle with cheese. Repeat layers of tortilla pieces, chicken and soup mixture, and cheese.

Cover and cook on low for 6 to 8 hours or high for 3 hours.

Cowgirl's Chicken Potpie

I wound up with quite a few cans of canned green peas, because they were cheap. The pea soup I devised was terrific (page 66) but then what? Chicken potpie, and I really do mean "pie"! Once again, Bisquick has proved to me that it should be a staple in every Cowgirl's pantry, especially if she has quite a few cans of peas.

Serves 6

JILL CHARLOTTE STANFORD

    1 (15-ounce) can green peas, drained
    1 (15-ounce) can mixed vegetables, drained
    1 cup cooked and diced chicken
    1 (10¾-ounce) can cream of chicken soup
    1 cup Bisquick
    ½ cup milk
    1 egg
    Salt and pepper to taste

Preheat the oven to 400°F.

In an ungreased 9-inch pie plate, stir the peas, mixed vegetables, chicken, and soup together.

In a medium bowl, stir in the Bisquick, milk, egg, and salt and pepper until blended. Pour into the pie plate.

Bake uncovered for about 30 minutes or until the crust is golden brown. Let the pie rest before cutting, about 5 minutes.

Southern Cowgirls' Crawfish Boil

Call them crayfish, crawfish, or crawdads—they are freshwater crustaceans that resemble and are related to lobsters. They are mostly found in brooks and streams where there is clean freshwater running. Most crayfish cannot tolerate polluted water. Now don't you feel better about them? But wait until you eat them!

Ginnie Bakersfield is a Cowgirl in Mississippi, raising registered Angus cattle. When she's not herding the cattle, she can be found crouched knee-deep in a stream that runs through her spread, capturing crawfish and putting them in a bucket of water for cooking up just a few minutes later. She says, "Live crawfish are the best! I think we 'raise' more crawfish than beef here. After they are cooked, just pinch the tails and suck the heads to eat. You can also cook crab, lobster, or shrimp this way."

Serves 12

    2 large onions, quartered
    10 large cloves garlic, halved
    2 lemons, quartered
    2 oranges, quartered
    5 large stalks celery, cut into chunks
    6 jalapeño peppers, halved and seeded
    ¼ cup black pepper
    ¼ cup seasoned salt
    10 pounds live crawfish, rinsed and kept alive in the bucket until you are ready
    to cook them

Place the onions, garlic, lemons, oranges, celery, and jalapeños in a 4- or 5-gallon pot. Season with pepper and seasoned salt. Add enough water to fill the pot ¾ full.

Bring to a hard boil over intense heat and allow to boil for 20 minutes.

Take a deep breath and add the crawfish. Cover and boil for 20 minutes, until the shells turn red.

Drain and eat.

Keep your lips red, your mind set and your hair long. Oh my darlin' cowgirl, keep your head up and your heart strong.

— Jennifer J. Denison

Freezer Chicken

The next time you go to that big warehouse store, buy the big package of chicken breasts. Put as many pieces of the raw (washed first) or frozen breasts you want (usually two or four) in a freezer bag. (For two chicken breasts, use a quart-size bag. For four chicken breasts, use a gallon-size bag.) You then add the marinade of your choice, turn the bag over and over to coat well, and freeze flat.

When it's time for dinner or lunch, thaw out a packet and remove the breasts. Put them in a baking dish with the marinade. Bake them in a preheated oven at 350°F for 45 minutes, turning over to coat them with the marinade. Grill them under a preheated broiler for 15 minutes per side, turning once, or put them in your Crock-Pot in the morning with the setting on low for an evening's supper.

Lemony Garlicky Marinade

For 4 chicken breasts (cut the recipe in half for 2 breasts)

In a bowl, whisk together:

  2 cloves garlic, chopped finely
  ¼ cup olive oil
  2 tablespoons chopped parsley
  3 tablespoons lemon juice
  ⅛ teaspoon pepper

Instead of marinating your chicken, why not make that delicious barbecue sauce on page 84?

Friday Night Fish *good!*

This is going to be your secret recipe. You will not tell a soul, ever, how you made this moist and delicious fish. No one will ever guess how you did this, except for Marjorie Rogers. Unless, of course, they buy this book and read the directions …

Serves 4

> 1 tablespoon vegetable oil, or any cooking spray
> Four pieces of fresh or frozen whitefish such as haddock or cod, about 8–10 ounces per person (a ½ pound each will do)
> ½ cup mayonnaise, the real stuff (not Miracle Whip)
> ½ cup bread crumbs, plain or seasoned
> 1 lemon, thinly sliced
> 1 cup white wine or water
> Salt and freshly ground pepper to taste

Preheat the oven to 375°F. *~ 25 min?*

Spray or coat with oil a 9 x 11-inch glass baking dish.

Lay the fish flat in the baking dish. Using a spatula, spread a layer of mayonnaise on the fish like you would on a sandwich, as thick or as thin as you like. (Me? Pretty thick!)

Sprinkle the coated fish with the bread crumbs, then lay the lemon slices on top. Pour the white wine or water all around the fish to add moisture, covering the bottom of the pan.

JILL CHARLOTTE STANFORD

Bake, uncovered, about 15 to 20 minutes or until the fish is done, when it's white in the middle, not opaque, and will flake easily.

Add salt and freshly ground pepper on top and chopped, fresh parsley if you feel like it.

Never tell a soul how you did this, because they will ask.

BEWARE: I ride horses which means I own pitchforks, have the strength to haul hay, and have the guts to scream at a half-ton animal after being kicked . . . you will NOT be a problem!

—Cowgirl Wisdom of the Day

Old-Fashioned Fried Chicken Breasts

Is there a better supper than fried chicken? Almost everyone will agree the breasts are the best part, so let's just do those, shall we? This is my sister Robin's recipe.

Serves 4

> 4 chicken breasts, bone in and skin on
> ¾ cup all-purpose flour
> 2 teaspoons lemon pepper
> 2 teaspoons Lawry's seasoned salt
> 1 teaspoon salt
> 2 eggs
> 2 tablespoons milk
> 2 tablespoons butter
> 2 tablespoons vegetable oil

Cut the chicken breasts in half crosswise. Prepare the breading by whisking together the flour, lemon pepper, seasoned salt, and salt in a shallow bowl.

Beat the eggs and milk together. Melt the butter in a heavy (cast iron preferred) skillet with the oil.

Dunk the chicken pieces in the egg mixture and then dredge in the flour mixture until well coated.

Place the chicken in the skillet skin-side down when the butter/oil mixture comes to a good bubble on medium-high heat. Cook to brown for 5 minutes. Turn the chicken pieces and cook to brown about 3 minutes more.

Turn the chicken down to medium-low and put a lid on the skillet, but don't put the lid down all the way. Leave some space for venting. Cook the chicken, turning often, for another 30 minutes. The smaller pieces will cook sooner than the larger ones.

Drain the cooked chicken pieces on paper towels and keep them in a warm oven at 200°F until all the pieces are done.

Serve with mashed potatoes and country gravy made with the drippings in your pan, about 3 or 4 tablespoons, as well as the "crumbles." Whisk in 3 or 4 tablespoons of flour until you have paste. Let the paste cook a few minutes, then add about 1 cup water and ½ cup milk all at once. Turn the heat to medium and keep whisking until the flour/fat mixture has dissolved and it starts to thicken. Keep whisking until it bubbles and cooks. You may need to add more water as it thickens to reach the consistency you want for the gravy. Traditionally, ground black pepper is added to the gravy.

Cowgirls have three main dishes: meats, vegetables, and breads. They use three spices: salt, pepper, and catsup.

—Anonymous

Tunafish Patties

very good fast

I am the daughter of a tugboat captain—not a tumbleweed in sight when I was growing up. Daddy and I both loved seafood. I would go with him to the beach on Puget Sound, and we would dig for the abundant clams. We brought them home and steamed them and ate them with melted butter. We also liked these tuna patties my mother made.

Makes 4 patties

2 (6-ounce) cans water-packed tuna, drained

2 teaspoons Dijon mustard

½ cup bread crumbs

1 teaspoon lemon zest

1 tablespoon lemon juice

1 tablespoon water

2 tablespoons chopped parsley

2 tablespoons chopped green onion

½ teaspoon Tabasco

Salt and freshly ground black pepper

1 egg

2 tablespoons olive oil

½ teaspoon butter

In a medium bowl, mix together the tuna, mustard, bread crumbs, lemon zest, lemon juice, water, parsley, green onions, and Tabasco. Sprinkle with salt and pepper. Taste the mixture before adding the egg to see if it needs more seasoning to your taste. Mix in the egg.

Divide the mixture into 4 parts. Form each part into a ball and then flatten into a patty. Put them on a plate with wax paper and chill for an hour. (You

We ate these patties with mayonnaise, but you could whip up a simple tartar sauce by combining mayonnaise and hamburger relish to taste.

can skip the chilling if you want—chilling just helps the patties stay together when you cook them.)

Heat the olive oil and a little butter (for taste) in a cast-iron or nonstick skillet on medium-high. Gently place the patties in the pan and cook until nicely browned, 3 to 4 minutes on each side.

If you want one thing too much it's likely to be a disappointment. The healthy way is to learn to like the everyday things, like soft beds and buttermilk—and feisty gentlemen.

—Larry McMurtry, Lonesome Dove

It's What's for Dinner Beef Short Ribs

This is a recipe you will thank your slow cooker for every time you make it, and I can assure you, the hands on the ranch will ask for it again and again. No slow cooker? A heavy Dutch oven or casserole dish with a lid, in the oven at 275°F, will do just fine.

Serves 4

½ cup all-purpose flour
Salt and pepper
2½ pounds beef short ribs
¼ cup butter
1 cup chopped onion
1 cup beef broth
¾ cup water
¾ cup brown sugar
2 tablespoons catsup
2 tablespoons Worcestershire sauce
2 tablespoons minced garlic
1 teaspoon chili powder

GLENBOW ARCHIVES #NA 5093-286

Put the flour, salt, and pepper in a bag. Add the ribs and shake them to coat.

Brown the ribs in the butter in a large skillet, then put them in the slow cooker or Dutch oven.

In the same skillet used to brown the ribs, brown the onion until it is nearly transparent, then add the remaining ingredients. Stir until it comes to nearly a boil.

Pour the mixture over ribs. Cover and cook on low for 9 hours.

Norma Jean's Barbecued Ribs

You might think you have a great recipe for barbecue sauce, but wait until you try this one. It's made with ingredients you might never have thought of!

Serves 2–4

2 cups V8 Original vegetable juice
1½ tablespoons white wine vinegar
1 cup catsup
1½ teaspoons A.1. Steak Sauce
1½ teaspoons Worcestershire sauce
2 tablespoons garlic powder
1½ cups brown sugar
Lemon juice to taste
2 racks meaty spare ribs

Mix all the ingredients (except the ribs) in a microwave-safe bowl. Microwave on high for 30 seconds to meld the flavors.

Brown the ribs on the grill or under a broiler before adding the sauce.

Place the browned ribs in a shallow baking dish lined with foil. Add ½ cup water.

Coat the ribs with the sauce, then cover with the foil. Bake for 2 to 2½ hours, until the meat pulls away from the bone. Brush the ribs with the sauce every ½ hour during cooking. Uncover the ribs for the last half-hour of cooking.

Pyrenees-Style Pickled Tongue

Cindy Forbes, the one-cowgirl band behind her business, Twist N Ties (see page 157), lives in Ronan, in northwest Montana, with her husband and children. She says, "We are an hour or so north of Missoula, and an hour or so south of Kalispell. We have 130 acres. We raise registered Angus cattle, and we grow our own hay and sell the excess. My mom got this recipe from old family friends that used to own Toll House Ranch in Caliente, California, Edna and Boyd Williams. That was maybe forty years ago … give or take! We eat this cold with crackers or in a sandwich with mustard and mayonnaise. There was nothing better than to go to the Kern County Fair, in Bakersfield, California, and have a tongue sandwich!"

I would add to this that in past times, no self-respecting ranch wife or cowgirl would let any part of the beef go to waste. In our modern lives, we forget that the heart, liver, and tongue were considered delicacies and kept back for the family when the beef was slaughtered. Try this recipe and I think you will agree. How do I know? My mother made this, too. And yes, I loved it! My sister Robin? Not so much.

Serves 6

1 beef tongue
½ cup olive oil
1 cup red wine vinegar
1 medium bunch fresh parsley, chopped
4 cloves garlic, peeled and sliced
½ teaspoon salt
¼ teaspoon pepper

Rinse the tongue, place in a large pot, and cover with water and salt. Bring to a boil, then reduce to a simmer for 2 to 3 hours until tender to a fork.

Remove the cooked tongue and plunge it into cold water. Remove it when it is cool enough to handle. Gently peel away the skin and any visible fat. Cover with plastic wrap and place in fridge to cool, overnight.

Make the marinade with the remaining ingredients in the list, adding any optional items like whole peppercorns.

Remove the cooled, firm, cooked tongue from the fridge and slice as thinly as possible (using an electric meat slicer is ideal). Arrange the thin-sliced tongue meat in a shallow glass or plastic container. Cover with the marinade and refrigerate for 1 to 3 days, turning occasionally.

When ready to serve, arrange the marinated meat on a serving platter.

You know you are a Cowgirl if . . . you have hay dust and dirt on every single pair of dress shoes you own!

Pulled Pork Parfait

If you didn't make it to the Snaffle Bit Futurity but heard about this offering at the lunch counter and wondered about it, wonder no more! This really *is* good, believe me. Odd, but good! My Volunteer Kitchen Testing Troops all asked if we couldn't try this just one more time.

The vendors use a clear plastic cup, so you can see the layers. I just use a deep soup bowl and let people dig in.

Bottom layer: hot baked beans
Next layer: barbecued pulled pork
Next layer: a dollop of barbecue sauce (See page 84 for a good one!)
Next: grated cheddar cheese
Then: more pulled pork
Top it all off with mashed potatoes.

Many grocery stores have all these ingredients that you can buy separately—saves time!

PHOTO BY ROBIN JOHNSON

How do you make barbecue pulled pork? Easy. Here's how:

Serves 6

- 1 2-pound pork tenderloin (pork shoulder or butt can also be used)
- 1 (12-ounce) can root beer
- 1 (18-ounce) bottle barbecue sauce, or make your own

Place the pork tenderloin in a slow cooker and pour the can of root beer over the meat. Cover and cook on low for 6 hours or until pork shreds easily with a fork when you test it.

After the pork has cooked, drain and discard the root beer. Shred the pork and place it back in the slow cooker. Pour the barbecue sauce over the pork and stir to combine. Serve immediately or keep warm in the slow cooker until ready to serve.

PHOTO BY ROBIN JOHNSON

You can also serve the pulled pork on hamburger buns for a terrific sandwich.

Saloon Meatballs

Out West, saloons always offered their patrons something to eat, like pickled eggs. The idea was that if the patrons had something in their stomachs, they wouldn't get as tipsy. If you are having a gathering in your own private saloon, I highly recommend these. Quick and easy to do!

Serves 4

> ½ cup catsup
> ½ cup brown sugar
> ¼ cup any good whiskey
> 1 teaspoon fresh lemon juice
> 1 teaspoon Worcestershire sauce
> 1 (1-pound) bag frozen meatballs, or 18–29 ping pong ball–size meatballs

In a medium bowl, combine all the ingredients except the meatballs.

Place the frozen meatballs in your Crock-Pot, and pour the whiskey sauce on top. Mix it up all around so each meatball is coated with the sauce.

Now turn up the heat to high. Leave it on high for about 1 hour, stirring a couple of times.

Once the meatballs have thawed, turn your Crock-Pot down to low. The meatballs are ready to serve—either straight from the Crock-Pot or you can transfer them to a deep dish.

You can also cook, and serve, these meatballs in a deep skillet that has been put on a trivet or hot pad to protect your table. Tip: Put a shot glass of toothpicks next to the serving piece and provide napkins.

Chicken 'n' Dumplings

awful good!

When the work's all done and it's time for an old-fashioned Sunday dinner, this is classic ranch and Cowgirl fixins. Special thanks to Rosemary Browne out there in Oklahoma for this. I loved it!

Serves 6

1 chicken, cut up in pieces, washed and dried
6 cups water, or to cover
2 stalks celery, chopped
1 carrot, chopped
1 medium onion, chopped
4 chicken bouillon cubes
1 teaspoon poultry seasoning
1 teaspoon garlic powder
1 teaspoon pepper
Salt to taste

For the dumplings:
1 cup all-purpose flour
2 teaspoons baking powder
1 teaspoon salt
⅔ cup milk
3 teaspoons butter, melted
1 teaspoon chopped parsley

Put the chicken pieces in a large pot with enough water to cover them completely. Add the celery, carrot, onion, bouillon cubes, poultry seasoning, garlic powder, and pepper. Bring to a boil, skimming the surface "foam" if necessary. Turn down the heat and simmer for 1 hour, covered, or until the chicken is tender.

Remove the chicken from the heat and let it sit. Taste the broth or gravy (see below) and add salt if you wish.

Mix the dumpling ingredients together until just moistened.

Bring the chicken back to a slow boil. Drop dumplings by tablespoons into the chicken and broth. Cover and cook for about 12 minutes, until the dumplings are cooked through.

If you want, make a gravy by stirring 4 tablespoons of flour into a cup of cold water, and then adding the flour/water to the hot chicken and broth. Stir until thickened.

Horses were never wrong. They always did what they did for a reason, and it was up to you to figure it out.

—Jeannette Walls, Half Broke Horses: A True-Life Novel

Divine Turkey

When my son, Charlie, was a little cowboy, he would not eat broccoli except in this casserole. I know a few grown-up cowboys and cowgirls who won't eat broccoli either except in this dish. Charlie called it Divine Turkey, and it was always served a few days after Thanksgiving, freeing up the turkey carcass for the soup I made the next day. It's fast and, yes, it uses cream of chicken soup, but when you have livestock to feed, not to mention a hungry family, this is a lifesaver with no leftovers. (You can use leftover chicken, too, and I have even run into it at a potluck with leftover ham as the meat. Cream of celery soup made it quite good!)

Serves 4

    4 cups cooked broccoli florets, drained
    2 cups leftover turkey, cut into cubes
    1 (10¾-ounce) can cream of chicken soup
    ½ cup milk
    ¼ teaspoon pepper
    ½ cup shredded cheddar cheese

Preheat the oven to 450°F.

In a 2-quart baking dish, spread out the broccoli and the turkey pieces.

In a small bowl, mix the soup, milk, and pepper. Pour this over the broccoli and turkey, then sprinkle the cheese evenly over it all.

Bake for 15 minutes or until the cheese is melted and bubbly.

Hildy's Swedish Meatballs

Hildegaard "Hildy" Larson looks like a Cowgirl and talks like a Cowgirl except when she's agreeing with you and she says "Ya." Her blue eyes and blonde hair give her away as well. Coming from Sweden, she has adapted to life in the Wild West and has adapted her family recipe for these heavenly meatballs, too.

Serves 4

For the meatballs:
>   1 small onion, chopped
>   1 egg
>   ¼ cup bread crumbs
>   2 tablespoons milk
>   ¾ teaspoon nutmeg
>   ¼ teaspoon allspice
>   ½ teaspoon salt
>   ⅛ teaspoon pepper
>   1 pound ground beef

For the sauce:
>   1 (10¾-ounce) can cream of mushroom soup, undiluted
>   ½ cup sour cream
>   ¼ cup milk
>   1 tablespoon dried parsley flakes

In a large bowl, combine the onion, egg, bread crumbs, milk, spices, and salt and pepper. Crumble the beef over the mixture and mix well, using your hands. Shape into 1-inch meatballs, about 24.

Place the meatballs in a shallow 1½-quart microwave-safe dish. Cover and microwave on high for 7½ minutes or until the meat is no longer pink. Drain and set aside, keeping warm.

In a saucepan, combine the soup, sour cream, milk, and parsley and stir and cook over medium heat until warm. Pour the sauce over the meatballs.

Serve with hot cooked egg noodles.

You know you are a Cowgirl if . . .
you walk into a room and someone
says, "What's in your hair?" Uh, hay.

County Fair Indian Tacos

Every year, most Cowgirls and Cowboys get the chores finished early and go to the county fair and rodeo. There is lots to see and do, livestock to admire, perhaps enter the rodeo, go up in the air on the Ferris wheel, and try your hand at darts to win a big teddy bear. But when you get hungry, and you always do, this is one of the booths you will stand in line for.

Serves 12

    12 frozen dinner rolls
    1 pound ground beef
    1 package taco seasoning mix
    ¼ cup water
    Cooking oil
    2 cups chopped iceberg lettuce
    1 tomato, chopped
    2 cups shredded cheddar cheese
    1 cup sliced black olives
    Taco sauce to taste
    Sour cream to taste

Place the frozen rolls on a greased cookie sheet. Let them thaw and rise until nearly doubled in size.

In the meantime, brown the ground beef, drain, and then add taco mix and water. Remove from heat and set aside.

Heat about 2 inches of cooking oil in a skillet or frying pan. Stretch the dinner

PHOTO BY ROBIN JOHNSON

roll dough quite thin and fry until golden brown, turning once. Drain on paper towels.

Top each taco with the seasoned meat mixture, and layer with lettuce, tomatoes, and cheese on top. Garnish with the sliced black olives, taco sauce, and a dollop of sour cream.

JILL CHARLOTTE STANFORD

Mustang-Fast Skillet Supper

It's the end of the day and the question is, "What to do for supper?" This! It's fast, fun, and really good.

Serves 4

1 (14½-ounce) can stewed tomatoes, undrained
½ cup water
1 (15½-ounce) can black beans, rinsed
1 cup instant brown rice, uncooked
1 cup corn, fresh or canned; if using canned, drain
1 (4-ounce) can green chiles, drained, washed, seeded, and chopped
½ teaspoon cumin
¼ teaspoon chili powder
Salt and pepper to taste

Combine all the ingredients except the salt and pepper in your largest skillet. Bring to a boil, then turn down the heat and simmer for 10 minutes or until all the liquid is absorbed.

Now add salt and pepper to taste. (You can also add leftover chicken or cubed ham if you want.)

Serve with tortilla chips and sour cream.

Tell me, what is it you plan to do with your one wild and precious life?

—*Mary Oliver*

Too Far from the Pizza Parlor Pizza Pockets

You will need a bundt pan. It will be worth it to buy one, if you don't already have one, because you will be making these again and again! The ridges of the cake pan allow these tasty morsels to cook through and not stick to the sides.

Serves 8 (But be sure you have a large salad to go along with this, because 1 per person is not enough.)

    5 tablespoons butter, divided
    ½ tablespoon dry Italian seasoning
    1 (16.3-ounce) tube refrigerated biscuits
    8 teaspoons pizza sauce
    1 cup grated or shredded mozzarella cheese (prepackaged is fine!)
    Any other topping you would like to add (I've used green peppers, mushrooms, and sliced olives.)

Preheat the oven to 350°F.

To prep your pan, spread 2 tablespoons of butter all around the bottom and sides. Sprinkle the dry Italian seasoning along the sides and bottom.

Open the tube of biscuits. Open the top of one biscuit and gently pull it apart. Stuff the inside with 1 teaspoon sauce, some cheese, and any toppings. Pinch the top back together to seal it back up. Place seam-side up, on its edge, in the pan.

Once you have all 8 of the biscuits stuffed, pour 3 tablespoons of melted butter on and over the tops. Bake for 15 to 20 minutes, until the tops are a rich golden brown color.

Remove from the oven and flip onto a serving platter.

Sunday Supper

"Supper" is a term for a meal taken in the late afternoon or early evening. Often, the pastor of the local church (which might be as far as 15 to 20 miles away) was asked to join everyone at the ranch house table, bringing a certain amount of propriety to the otherwise rowdy crew and family. The cook, usually the wife, had to come up with something special.

I have a treasured piece of yellowing paper with a menu written in pencil by an unknown woman for what she has titled at the top SUNDAY SUPPER.

> Boiled chikin [*sic*]
> Salt ham
> Green beans
> My rolls
> Pickle relish
> 2 pies
> Cream if the cow gives

We can assume that she had to kill and pluck and clean the chicken. She already had the ham in the smokehouse. The green beans were either fresh from the garden (and I would bet my boots there was a piece of salt pork in the water) or canned. Her rolls were, I'll bet, very good, and she had to bake them in a woodstove oven. She made the pickle relish, and I think she was proud of it. What were the pies? Dried apple? Mincemeat? Were there berries? And that cow was clearly vexing her! I'll bet she had a tablecloth washed and ironed, and the children were scrubbed behind the ears. The ranch hands were admonished to be on their *best* behavior, which most likely rendered them speechless.

*An occasional cowgirl, in fringed buckskin
or riding costume, strolls by with that
unobtrusiveness which is a salient characteristic
of these range women.*

*—Charles Wellington Furlong, reporter at the
Pendleton Round-Up, 1916*

Wild Game

Not so long ago, "wild game" was the staple along with beef and mutton. Here are some tasty ways to prepare what you have to work pretty damn hard to get!

PHOTO COURTESY OF NICOLE CARTER

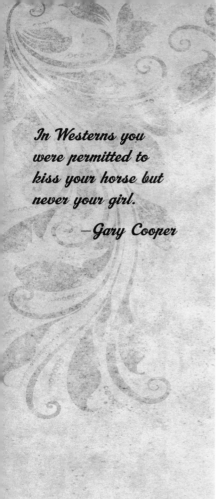
Juniper Chili

Nicole Carter lives in Homedale, Idaho. She has two darling children and a job "with the Feds," she says. But this Cowgirl is also an avid hunter. That is not Goth makeup she's wearing on page 101, it's camo so the game can't see her as well. She says, "I shot my first whitetail, a 4 x 5 buck, with a Remington 270. I like to hunt turkey and pheasants, too. I made this chili for a chili cook-off and came in second!"

You can make this with either elk or deer burger or beef stew meat.

Serves 6

1½ cups great northern beans
1½ cups white butter beans
1½ cups white kidney beans
1½ cups white shoepeg (white kernel) corn
1½ cups black-eyed peas
2 cups beef broth
1 medium sweet onion, chopped
1 stalk celery, chopped
1–2 tablespoons roasted garlic
1 pound elk or deer burger or stew meat
2–3 cups torn or chopped fresh cilantro
1–2 tablespoons cumin
Salt and fresh ground pepper
Secret ingredient: 1 tablespoon or to taste juniper berry and peppercorn rub that you order from www.wildeats.com. Just pour directly into Crock-Pot. (It's a blend of African black peppercorns, juniper berries, salt, and garlic.)

Mix all the ingredients in a Crock-Pot and cook on low for 6 hours.

Elk Heart and Liver

Caprice Madison lives up in the Flattops Wilderness in Colorado. She has a Facebook page called "Mountain Woman." Curious, I "friended" her. She said she was going out hunting, and I asked if she would share a recipe with me. She replied, "My husband and I hunt here in Colorado. The game meat we get sustains us through winter. This is a great favorite when we get back to the cabin."

> 1 fresh elk heart, washed
> 1 fresh elk liver, washed and peeled

Cut 'em up. Soak 'em in salt water for a day or two.

Roll 'em in flour with salt and pepper to taste and fry 'em up.

She went on: "My husband guided a hunter for a bull elk this year. The first day he shot too high. Then the next day my husband took him to a place to 'stand' and the hunter said, 'I can't walk that far.' The next day (this went on for 7 days) they rode out and again my husband had him in some elk—about 14—but the hunter didn't see them so my husband said, 'Well, why don't we just go scatter 'em?' On another day he missed his shot and my husband said, 'Reload!' but the hunter said, 'I don't have my ammo with me, it's on my horse.' FINALLY on the last day his hunter got a bull! We ate the heart and liver. Instead of saying 'Pass the salt and pepper' up here, it's 'Pass the ammo.'"

A Honey of a Pheasant Dish

Our friend Peter Voorhies was an avid bird hunter, but had no wife to cook the pheasants and ducks (and the occasional goose) he bagged. Our deal was he would provide the birds and a bottle of wine, and I would cook the meal. The only problem was I had no idea how to cook game. I learned fast! Pheasant is a favorite of mine now, but I learned the hard way that it is a very dry bird with precious little fat on it.

Serves 2

> 2 pheasants, cleaned and dressed (Be sure to check for shot—they can break a tooth.)
> Enough honey to cover both birds
> ¼ cup lemon juice
> Salt and pepper
> 1 lemon, halved
> Garlic powder to taste
> ½ teaspoon thyme (¼ teaspoon per bird)
> 2 slices bacon, one for each bird

Preheat the oven to 400°F. Put the pheasants in a baking dish.

Spread honey over each bird, including the legs, thighs, and wings. Pour the lemon juice over the pheasants. Season the cavities generously with salt, pepper, and half a lemon each. Season the skin with salt, pepper, garlic powder, and the thyme. Lay a bacon strip lengthwise over each bird.

Put the baking dish in the oven on the second shelf up from the bottom. Bake until the juices run clear when you prick the skin of the pheasant, about 30 minutes.

Rabbit Stew

In the early days, the intrepid pioneer women had little choice but to snare or shoot the abundant rabbits out on the prairies to feed their families. Annie Oakley kept her family well supplied with rabbits when she was a young girl and sharpened her skill at shooting at the same time. Many years later, this recipe is still as good now as it was way back then.

If you are so inclined, you can substitute squirrel for the rabbit. Or a chicken if you miss your shot.

Serves 4–6

For the marinade:

½ cup vinegar

2 tablespoons salt

2 cloves garlic, peeled and minced

Enough cold water to cover the rabbit

For the stew:

1 rabbit, cut up like a fryer chicken

1 large onion, cut in quarters

1 small green pepper, cut in quarters

1–2 stalks celery, sliced

2 cloves garlic, chopped

Salt and pepper

½ teaspoon sage

1 tablespoon dried parsley

1–2 carrots, cut into rounds

3 tablespoons catsup

Cayenne pepper to taste

1 cup liquid (It can be cider, tomato juice, or water.)

Mix the marinade ingredients in a wide, shallow pan.

Put the rabbit meat in the marinade. Refrigerate overnight.

Brown the rabbit, with the prepared vegetables, in a hot skillet for 5 to 10 minutes.

Place the browned rabbit and vegetables and the remaining ingredients in a Crock-Pot or Dutch oven. Cover and cook on low for 8 to 10 hours.

Horses live in the moment; now there may be some things from their past that give you some trouble in the moment, but you have to fix it going forward, not backward.

—Buck Brannaman

Slow Cooker Venison

The word *venison* means "meat from a deer." It comes to us from Middle English that began as the Old French *venesoun,* which can be traced all the way back to the Latin *venatio,* or "hunting." All of which goes to show you that we have been consuming "meat from a deer" for a very long time.

Serves 8

1 (10½-ounce) can cream of mushroom soup, undiluted
1 cup Cabernet Sauvignon or dry red wine (optional)
2 beef bouillon cubes, crumbled
3 cloves garlic, peeled and minced
1 large onion, diced
1 (8-ounce) can sliced mushrooms, drained
1 tablespoon Tabasco sauce
2 teaspoons thyme, crumbled
3 pounds venison roast (or lean beef roast if the hunt didn't go so well)
6 large potatoes, quartered
8 carrots, peeled and cut into 4-inch-long pieces (optional)
3–4 tablespoons cornstarch (optional)
¼ cup water (optional)

In a Crock-Pot, or a deep and heavy casserole dish with a lid, add the soup, wine, bouillon, garlic, onion, mushrooms, Tabasco, and thyme. Stir to mix well.

Add the roast. Turn it several times to coat. Turn the Crock-Pot on high and cook 4 to 6 hours or until the meat is just tender.

Cook the potatoes and carrots in boiling salted water and until fork tender. Drain.

Take the roast out of the Crock-Pot and place it on a platter. Put the starch in a cup and add the water to it, stirring with a fork. Whisk this into the hot liquid in the Crock-Pot. Stir until gravy thickens.

Serve with potatoes and carrots, or cooked noodles or rice.

30 miles to water, 20 miles to wood, 10 miles to hell and I gone there for good.

—Carved on a deserted shack near Chadron, Nebraska

Texas Venison Meatballs

Cowgirl Audrey Clossen says, "Depending on how much you like the 'wild meats,' this recipe can be adjusted for more or less meat or seasonings. We are free and easygoing spirits in Texas!"

Serves 4

> 1 pound finely ground venison
> ½ pound finely ground pork (or wild hog if you bagged one!)
> 1 cup grated Romano cheese
> 1 teaspoon salt
> ¼ teaspoon pepper
> 1 cup bread crumbs
> 1–2 cloves garlic, peeled and finely chopped
> 1 tablespoon chopped fresh oregano
> 3 tablespoons chopped fresh basil
> 2 eggs

Preheat the oven to 350°F.

Combine all the ingredients and mix well.

Shape the mixture into balls. Place on a baking sheet that has been sprayed with cooking spray.

Bake the meatballs for 20 minutes. If you make large meatballs, it will take a little longer.

Put the cooked meatballs in a serving bowl when baking is complete, and place in the refrigerator. About 2 hours prior to dinnertime, pop the meatballs into any red spaghetti sauce and warm them before serving. They can also be frozen for future use.

Wild Hog Meatballs and Gravy

Audrey Clossen lives in Spring Branch, Texas. When I asked her if she was a Cowgirl, she replied, "Jill, I am a cowgirl in spirit only, although I DO have 'Should've Been a Cowboy' by Toby Keith for a ringtone on my phone. I run back and forth from the Hill Country to the beautiful Gulf of Mexico and the islands there. Sometimes we really DO wear cowboy boots!" That works for me! No wild hog handy? Use ground pork from the grocery store. These meatballs are simply out of this world.

Serves 6

For the meatballs:

    2 cups bread crumbs

    ½ cup milk

    1 pound finely ground wild pork (or market pork)

    1 pound finely ground beef

    3 eggs

    1 cup chopped yellow onions

    1–2 tablespoons ground cardamom

    Salt and pepper to taste

    1 cup butter, divided

    6 cups sliced yellow onions

    ½ cup sugar

    1 sprig parsley

For the gravy:

    3 cups beef broth

    2 cups heavy cream

    1 teaspoon ground nutmeg

    1 teaspoon ground allspice

    ¼ teaspoon cinnamon

    ¼ teaspoon cloves

3½ tablespoons cornstarch
¼ cup water

In a large mixing bowl, soak the bread crumbs in the milk for 5 minutes. Mix in the meat, eggs, and chopped onions. Season with cardamom and salt and pepper to taste. Roll into 1- to 1½-inch meatballs.

Sauté the meatballs in ¼ cup butter for approximately 20 minutes.

In a separate skillet, sauté the sliced onions with ¼ cup butter and sugar until caramelized, about 10 to 15 minutes. Season with salt and pepper to taste.

Remove the meatballs and the onions from both pans, and place on separate plates.

To make the gravy, deglaze both sauté pans with the remaining ½ cup butter and the beef broth, scraping up the browned bits. Cook over high heat for 1 minute.

PHOTO BY ROBIN JOHNSON

Place the contents of both sauté pans into one large pot, and stir in the cream and the caramelized onions. Season with nutmeg, allspice, cinnamon, and cloves. Bring to a simmer.

Mix the cornstarch and water together, and with a whisk, mix the slurry into the cream sauce. Add the meatballs and simmer approximately 20 to 30 minutes.

Serve on top of egg noodles or a slice of bread and garnish with parsley.

Florence Hughes Randolph

Born in 1878 and standing 4 feet 6 inches tall, Florence Hughes Randolph was a giant at heart. She started trick riding at the age of thirteen, and made more than 500 rodeo appearances. She was a ten-time World Champion Cowgirl Trick Rider and Bronc Rider and hosted her own Wild West show, "Princess Mohawk's Wild West Hippodrome." Wild West shows, motorcycle racing, doubling for movie stars—Florence did it all! She died in 1971 after a long and daring life.

COURTESY OF MADONNA ESKEW PUMPHREY

Sauces, Salsas, and Rubs

Sometimes, it's the little things that make a meal or a dish sparkle.
Especially if you have made it yourself.

PHOTO COURTESY OF TED MOOMAW, OLD BUCKING HORSE MUSEUM

Coffee Bean Steak Rub

Cowgirl On Coffee sent this to me. High-octane good!

Makes 1 rub, or ¼ cup

> 1 tablespoon whole coffee beans
> 1 tablespoon white peppercorns
> ⅛ teaspoon paprika
> ½ tablespoon garlic powder
> ½ tablespoon sea salt
> 1 tablespoon all-purpose seasoning

Combine all the ingredients in a blender or a spice or coffee grinder. Finely grind the mixture.

Rub onto your favorite steak or tri-tip 30 minutes or more prior to cooking.

Summertime or Anytime Peach Salsa

I love peach salsa! You can dip tortilla chips in it, of course, but how about serving it on pancakes or waffles in the middle of winter? That will start your day off! When you are chopping jalapeños, remove the seeds and veins from the peppers and *always* wear gloves to avoid mistakenly rubbing your eyes and *owwww!* If you want salsa with a lot of heat, then leave the seeds in.

Makes 4 pint or 8 half-pint jars of hot stuff!

6 ripe peaches, peeled, pitted, and diced
½ cup white vinegar
1¼ cups chopped sweet onion
4 jalapeño peppers, chopped
1 red bell pepper, seeded and chopped
½ cup loosely packed, finely chopped cilantro
2 tablespoons honey
1 clove garlic, peeled and finely chopped
1½ teaspoons cumin
½ teaspoon cayenne pepper
4 pint or 8 half-pint jars (I prefer Bell), sterilized

Combine all the ingredients in a saucepan and bring to a boil over medium heat, stirring the entire time so it does not scorch. Reduce the heat and continue boiling gently until it's slightly thickened.

Ladle the hot salsa mix into the washed and sterilized jars. Leave a little room on top for expansion.

Wipe the jar rims and then tighten on the lids. Put the filled jars in a large pot filled with water that has been brought to a boil and then allowed to simmer.

The half-pint jars make great gifts wrapped with a little red raffia.

Be sure the jars are completely covered. Bring the water back to a boil and process the salsa for 15 minutes.

Remove the jars and place them on a folded dish towel on the counter to cool completely. Then listen for the "ping" of each successfully sealed jar when you tap on the top of the lid.

You know you are a Cowgirl if . . . there is dust on the dress clothes that you very rarely wear because you have Wranglers for every occasion.

Some Like It Hot Sauce

A word of caution: The jalapeño has a heat level that varies from mild to hot depending on cultivation and preparation. When preparing jalapeños, your hands should not come in contact with your eyes, as this leads to painful burning and redness. Some people wear latex or vinyl gloves while cutting, skinning, or seeding jalapeños.

That being said, this is a great hot sauce that will blow your boots off!

Makes 4 cups

> 1 teaspoon vegetable oil
> 18 fresh jalapeño peppers, seeded and sliced
> 3 cloves garlic, minced
> 1 cup minced sweet onion
> ¾ teaspoon salt
> 2 cups water
> 1 cup distilled white vinegar

In a medium glass or enamel-lined saucepan (not stainless steel or aluminum) over high heat, combine the oil, jalapeños, garlic, onion, and salt. Sauté for 4 minutes.

Add the water and cook for 20 minutes, stirring often. Remove from the heat and allow the sauce to cool to room temperature.

Transfer the sauce to a food processor or a blender and puree until smooth. With the processor or the blender running, slowly add the vinegar.

Pour the sauce into a sterilized jar with a tight lid. Keep refrigerated.

Cowgirl's Homemade Tomato Sauce

My sister, Robin, and I went to a farmers' market and bought a lot of organic Roma tomatoes. *A lot.* We went back to her place and peeled and chopped and canned them for *hours.* The result was a bounty of pint-size glass jars filled with wonderful, bright red tomatoes just asking to have things happen to them all winter long. Here is just one of the things I did with a jar, which equals 8 small Roma tomatoes.

Serves 2

 1 tablespoon butter
 8 small Roma tomatoes, peeled and diced
 ¼ cup chopped fresh or dried basil
 1 teaspoon olive oil
 1 teaspoon garlic salt
 Salt and freshly ground black pepper to taste
 1 tablespoon all-purpose flour
 ¼ cup water
 1 clove garlic, diced

Melt the butter in a large skillet over medium heat. Cook the tomatoes in the melted butter until they begin to fall apart, about 5 to 7 minutes. (If you are using your own home-canned tomatoes, or a can of whole tomatoes, just heat them in the butter.)

Add the basil, olive oil, garlic salt, salt, and pepper.

Slowly stir the flour into the mixture and cook until it begins to thicken, about 5 to 7 minutes.

JILL CHARLOTTE STANFORD

Stir the water through the mixture to break up any lumps of flour. Mix the garlic into the sauce and simmer another 5 minutes.

Serve hot over any pasta.

Don't let the lipstick fool you.
She can go from makeup to mud in three seconds flat.

—Anonymous

Desserts and Sweets

For many Cowgirls, there is *Dessert* and then everything else at a meal. Go ahead! Help yourself! Seconds are always allowed at a Cowgirl's table.

Blueberries, peaches, or other fruits can be substituted for the raspberries.

Branding Cobbler

Out in Buffalo, South Dakota, Melissa and Ty Fowler run the Grubbing Hoe Ranch. Every day is a busy day featuring cattle and horses. Melissa does all the cooking for the crews. "Here is one of my favorite branding recipes," she says. "Everyone just loves it!"

Serves 8

2 cups raspberries
2 cups blackberries
1 cup sugar
Zest of half a lemon
Squeeze of lemon
2 cups granola (any kind, but Melissa makes hers from scratch, and that recipe follows)
½ cup brown sugar
1 cup all-purpose flour
1 teaspoon cinnamon
½ teaspoon sea salt
½ cup butter

Preheat the oven to 350°F.

In a large bowl, toss the berries, sugar, lemon zest, and squeeze of lemon.

In another bowl, mix the granola, brown sugar, flour, cinnamon, sea salt, and butter and, with your fingers, rub

COURTESY OF MELISSA FOWLER

the butter into the mixture until it resembles small pebbles. Put the mixture in the fridge for 15 minutes or so to let it harden back up a little.

Scoop the berries evenly into a cake pan or into individual ramekins. Top with the granola mixture (recipe follows).

Bake for 45 minutes to 1 hour. Serve warm—it's great with a scoop of vanilla ice cream!

If you're fixin' to get yourself a good stallion, don't go lookin' in the donkey corral.

—Ciji Ware, Cottage by the Sea

MJ's Granola

This is the granola Melissa makes to use on the cobbler (see page 122), but you can also substitute your favorite brand from the grocery store if you need to save a little time.

Makes approximately 15 cups

> 3 cups sliced almonds
> 1 cup honey
> ½ cup brown sugar
> 2 teaspoons cinnamon
> ½ teaspoon nutmeg
> ½ teaspoon sea salt
> 1 cup apple juice
> 10 cups oats
> 2–3 cups dried fruit (currants, blueberries, raspberries, cranberries, or a mixture)

Preheat the oven to 300°F.

Spread the almonds on a cookie sheet and bake until light brown. Set aside in a bowl.

Put the honey, brown sugar, cinnamon, nutmeg, sea salt, and apple juice in a saucepan on low heat. Cook only until the brown sugar melts and the rest of the ingredients come together, about 5 minutes.

Put the oats in a bowl. Pour the honey mixture over the oats and mix well to make sure that all the oats are well-coated. Spread out on cookie sheets (with rims) into a thin layer (about ¼ inch or less) so the granola can dry out.

Bake for 45 minutes to 1 hour, checking every 10 minutes or so and stirring it around so it will crisp. Turn off the heat and let the granola cool completely. Once cool, mix the granola with the almonds and dried fruit. It will keep nicely in an airtight container in the fridge for about a month.

Angel Cake

This is so easy, it is ridiculous. It's not only what Cowgirls like, it's what they make, serve, and eat!

In an ungreased 9 x 13-inch pan, mix together:

    1 box of angel food cake mix (dry)
    1 20- or 22-ounce can of fruit pie filling, any flavor
    (I liked the blueberry.)

Bake at 350°F for 28 to 30 minutes. It will puff up.

That's it!

Serve while still warm, topped with vanilla ice cream.

Aunt Pearl's Red Velvet Cake

Charmain Vaughn was asked to head up a heroic undertaking—a cookbook to benefit a horse camp with recipes submitted by members of horsecity. com, the largest site for horse enthusiasts on the web. Needless to say, the recipes flooded her desk. I was asked to write the foreword to the cookbook. Somehow, with all she had to do, Charmain managed to get one of her favorite recipes in the book. She says, "This recipe came from my Aunt Pearl. You could bet if there was a church social or a family reunion, Aunt Pearl's Red Velvet Cake was there! She would be so proud to be in your book, too!"

Serves 8

> 2 cups sugar
> 2 cups Wesson Vegetable Oil
> 2 eggs
> 2 teaspoons cocoa
> 1 teaspoon vanilla
> 1 (4-ounce) bottle red food coloring
> 1 teaspoon white vinegar
> 2½ cups self-rising cake flour
> 1 teaspoon salt
> 1 cup buttermilk
> Cream Cheese Icing (recipe below)
> 1 cup chopped nuts

Preheat the oven to 350°F.

Cream the sugar and oil until smooth. Add the eggs, one at a time, and blend well. Add the cocoa, vanilla, and red coloring. Last of all, add the vinegar. Mix well.

In a separate bowl, sift the flour and salt. Add them alternately with the buttermilk to the wet ingredients until all are well blended.

Grease and flour three 8-inch cake pans. Divide the cake mixture evenly between the pans. Bake until a toothpick comes out clean from the center of each layer or when the edges pull away slightly from the sides of the pans, about 40 minutes.

Cool the cakes on a wire rack before frosting, then ice each layer with icing, including the top, and sprinkle the chopped nuts on the top. Ice the sides. Aunt Pearl says "ice" not frost—I like that.

Cream Cheese Icing

1 stick (½ cup) unsalted butter, room temperature
1 (8-ounce) package cream cheese, room temperature
1 (1-pound) box powdered sugar
1 teaspoon vanilla

Cream the butter and cream cheese until smooth.

Add the powdered sugar ¼ cup at a time, and beat until smooth. Add the vanilla and beat again.

Down-and-Dirty Toffee Tiramisu

Jennifer Denison, Senior Editor and Cowboy Culture Editor for *Western Horseman* magazine, and a friend started having dinner-and-movie nights and thought it would be fun to have themed dinners. For the Italian dinner night, Jenn was assigned to bring dessert. Tiramisu was the natural choice, but she knew it can be hard to make. "I found recipes for chocolate mousse and traditional tiramisu in old copies of *Southern Living* magazine," she says. "I combined the recipes and did a little experimenting to come up with this easy recipe." You will be glad she did.

Ciao!

Serves 8

1½ tablespoons instant coffee granules
¼ cup warm water
1 (10.75-ounce) premade pound cake
1 (8-ounce) package cream cheese, softened
½ cup powdered sugar
½ cup chocolate syrup
1 (12-ounce) container frozen whipped topping, thawed and divided
2 (1.4-ounce) toffee bars, coarsely chopped

Stir together the coffee and water until coffee has dissolved. Let it cool.

Cut the cake into 14 slices, then cut each slice in half, crosswise. Place the slices in the bottom of and overlapping up the sides of a 9-inch pie plate. Drizzle the coffee over the cake slices.

Beat the cream cheese, sugar, and chocolate syrup at medium speed with an electric mixer until smooth. Add 2½ cups whipped topping, and beat until light and fluffy.

PHOTO COURTESY OF JENNIFER DENISON

Spread the mixture over the cake. Dollop the remaining whipped topping in the center of the pie. Sprinkle the chopped toffee bars on top of the pie.

Cover and chill for 8 hours.

Florilla's Best Gingerbread Cake

Florilla Whitley lived on a small holding outside of Candor, New York, and became a Civil War widow at thirty-one years of age. Her husband, John, came home in May of 1865, having contracted malaria in the field. He applied for an invalid pension at the end of September and died on January 1, 1866—just eight months after he returned.

John's death changed Florilla's life forever. There were many "cowgirls" created by the war back then: They were widowed and alone but they soldiered on—what choice did they have? The small notebook of hers where this recipe comes from had more than the recipes in it: There are also her notations on her budgets—I'm sure there wasn't much money. She notes what she sold (eggs and produce) and what she bought ("boys Christmas"). Strong women back then—I'm sure they surprised themselves—but they took no pleasure or pride in it because they were forever heartsick.

I am proud to say that Florilla was my great-great-grandmother. My sister, Robin, has put her simple recipes into a lovely little book, word for word.

Original recipe:
   2 cups sweet cream
   2 eggs well beaten
   1 cup brown sugar
   4 cups flour
   1 cup molasses
   Heaping teaspoon soda
      dissolved in a little milk
   Heaping teaspoon ginger
   If liked, a little nutmeg or
      cinnamon

Bake an hour or until done in a slow oven.

PHOTO BY ROBIN JOHNSON

Revised recipe:

- 2 eggs
- 1 cup brown sugar
- 1½ teaspoons baking soda
- 1 tablespoon milk
- 1 cup molasses
- 2 cups heavy cream
- 4 cups all-purpose flour
- 2 teaspoons ground ginger
- ½ teaspoon cinnamon

Preheat the oven to 350°F. Grease and flour a standard Bundt pan.

With an electric mixer, beat the eggs well, then add the brown sugar. Beat on high until light and fluffy.

In a small bowl, "melt," or dissolve, the baking soda with the milk, then add the molasses. Stir until combined. Let this sit while you add the heavy cream to the egg mixture, then add the molasses mixture.

Whisk the flour, ginger, and cinnamon together and add all at once to the wet ingredients. Using a spoon, stir together until just well combined.

Pour the batter into the prepared pan and bake for 45 to 50 minutes, or until a toothpick comes out clean when tested.

Serve with whipped cream. If you have it, add some chopped candied ginger. Florilla would have liked that.

Ice Cream in a Bag

Nothing says "summer" quite like homemade ice cream. Forget having to turn the crank of an old-fashioned ice cream maker (which takes forever) or having to drive 20 miles down a dusty road to get ice cream that will melt before you get back to the ranch. This is quick, fun, and very good!

Serves 1

2 tablespoons sugar
1 cup half-and-half
½ teaspoon vanilla extract
1 pint-size Ziploc bag
½ cup salt (The bigger the granules, the better. Sea salt works best.)
Enough ice cubes to fill a gallon-size bag about half full
1 gallon-size Ziploc bag

Combine the sugar, half-and-half, and vanilla extract in the pint-size bag and seal it tightly.

Place the salt and ice in the gallon-size bag, then place the sealed smaller bag inside. Seal the larger bag.

Now shake the bags until the mixture hardens (about 5 minutes). Feel the small bag to determine when it's done. It will be like soft-serve.

Take the smaller bag out of the larger one. Add mix-ins like diced fresh peaches or chocolate chips ground fine, and eat the ice cream right out of the bag. Easy cleanup, too!

Pendleton Whisky Peach Cobbler

Eric Williams, wagon boss of the Texas Stampede Chuck Wagon in Dallas, offers this out-of-this-world cobbler as well as a little Texas culinary advice.

Serves 8

For the cobbler:

1 gallon peaches (preferably Del Monte brand); remove 2½ cups of juice and save, and break peach slices in half

1¼ cups sugar

1¼ cups brown sugar

⅓ cup butter

2 teaspoons almond extract

2 teaspoons vanilla butter extract

¼ teaspoon cinnamon

¼ teaspoon nutmeg

1 teaspoon salt

½ cup Pendleton Canadian Whisky

½ cup cornstarch

For the crust:

3 cups all-purpose flour

½ teaspoon salt

1 cup butter-flavored Crisco

1 egg

¾ cup cold water

For the egg wash:

1 egg

½ cup milk

Sugar and cinnamon to sprinkle on top

Preheat the oven to 375°F. Since you've already opened the Pendleton Whisky, make yourself a Pendleton cocktail to enhance your cooking experience. As we say on the Texas Stampede Chuck Wagon, "We like to use a lot of Pendleton Canadian Whisky when we're cookin'…sometimes we even put some in the food."

In a large pan (you might want to spray it with cooking spray to help with the cleanup), mix all the cobbler ingredients together with the exception of the cornstarch. Place the mixture over heat and bring to a boil, stirring frequently. Let boil for 3 to 5 minutes, then reduce heat until peaches are tender. If you're concerned about the alcohol in the cobbler, don't be; it will evaporate, leaving the wonderful smooth flavor or the Pendleton Whisky.

In a small bowl, mix the cornstarch with a small amount of the drained peach juice to make a smooth paste. Slowly add the cornstarch to thicken the cobbler. Stir constantly and pour slowly to avoid lumps. Use as much as needed to thicken the mixture.

Pour the peaches into a greased pan and let cool slightly. On the wagon, we cook our cobbler in a 16-inch Dutch oven so you will have to gauge what size pan you need for cooking at home. This probably makes enough to fill two 9 x 13-inch baking pans.

To make the crust, mix the flour and salt together in a large bowl. Cut the shortening into small pieces (¼ x ¼ inch). Add the pieces to the dry mix and work with your fingers until all of the pieces are coated with flour and the mixture resembles a coarse meal. Do not overwork the dough or it may be tough.

In a measuring bowl, crack the egg and add cold water until mixture equals ¾ cup. For a flakier crust, you can add a small amount (3 teaspoons) of lemon juice or white vinegar before adding the water. Pour the liquid over the dry ingredients and mix well. Only mix enough to bring it all together; again, overworking can make the crust tough.

Form the dough into a ball or 2-inch-thick patty and place in the refrigerator for 15 to 20 minutes to allow fat to re-chill. The crust can be made in advance and kept in the refrigerator.

Roll out the dough and cover the peach mixture. Mix an egg wash (egg and water or egg and milk) and brush over the crust. Sprinkle cinnamon sugar over the entire crust. Cut a couple of slits in the crust to release steam, and bake in 375°F oven until the crust is golden brown (approxi-

JILL CHARLOTTE STANFORD

mately 20 to 25 minutes). If you prefer to have a bottom crust, just make two crust recipes and place one in the pan and brown in the oven before adding the peach mixture and top crust.

Once the crust is golden brown, remove the cobbler from the oven and let cool for a short time before serving. This is one peach cobbler that you won't want to serve with ice cream. You won't want to do anything to dilute the wonderful flavor of this Pendleton Whisky Peach Cobbler.

"Let 'er buck!"

Autumn Harvest Pumpkin Bars

When summer has left the country and fall is looking in the windows, stoke up the fire, heat up some spiced apple cider on the stove, and make these wonderful pumpkin bars, courtesy of Cowgirl Lindsey Martinez.

Makes approximately 12 bars

4 eggs
1⅔ cups sugar
1 cup vegetable oil
1 (15-ounce) can pumpkin
2 cups all-purpose flour
2 teaspoons baking powder
1 teaspoon salt
1 teaspoon baking soda
2 teaspoons cinnamon

Preheat the oven to 350°F.

In a large bowl, beat together the eggs, sugar, vegetable oil, and pumpkin. Stir in the flour, baking powder, salt, baking soda, and cinnamon.

Spread in a greased 9 x 13 x 2-inch glass pan. Bake for 25 to 30 minutes or until golden brown on top.

Let cool on a rack while you make the frosting.

Frosting

    1 (8-ounce) package cream cheese
    ¼ cup margarine, softened
    1 teaspoon vanilla
    1½ cups powdered sugar

Beat the cream cheese until smooth. Add the margarine and vanilla, and gradually beat in the powdered sugar until the frosting is fluffy.

Lick the paddles of the mixer and the bowl.

You know you are a Cowgirl if . . .
you have had to kill a rattlesnake
in the garden in your party dress.

Saturday Nite Popcorn

The horses are unsaddled and fed; the dogs are inside with you by the fire. You have a really good video to watch, and here is what you will be snacking on. Go ahead! It's just you and the dogs, and they are not telling a soul. I'm not either.

> 3 bags microwave popcorn
> 2 sticks (1 cup) butter
> 1 (16-ounce) bag
>   marshmallows
> 1 cup brown sugar

Pop the popcorn, one bag at a time. Put the popcorn in a large bowl and take out the unpopped kernels.

In another bowl, microwave the butter, marshmallows, and brown sugar for 2½ minutes. Take out and stir. Microwave again for 1 minute. Repeat until it becomes thin enough to easily pour over the popcorn.

Mix it all together, grab some napkins, hit the "play" button, and you are welcome!

Rhubarb Custard Squares

In the old days, no farm or ranch garden was without rhubarb. A major source of vitamins and a hardy plant that dies down in the summer only to spring up in the spring, rhubarb was considered a tonic after a long winter. Its season is short, so make the best of it. Besides the usual pie or jam, try it this way.

Makes 12 squares

> 1 cup butter, softened
> 2 cups all-purpose flour
> ¼ teaspoon salt
> 2 tablespoons sugar
> 5 cups rhubarb, washed, peeled, and chopped

For the custard:
> 1¾ cups sugar
> ½ teaspoon salt
> ¼ cup all-purpose flour
> 4 eggs

Preheat the oven to 350°F. Grease a glass 9 x 13-inch pan.

Combine the softened butter, flour, salt, and sugar in a large bowl. Using a fork, a pastry cutter, or if you are a modern Cowgirl, your food processor, mix it together until it is crumbly.

Press into the pan, making sure it goes up the sides. Cover with the chopped rhubarb.

In a medium bowl, beat the sugar, salt, flour, and eggs together. Pour the custard over the rhubarb/crust.

Bake in the center of the oven for at least 1 hour. The top should have a slight brown crust, like apple crisp.

Best. Fruitcake. Ever.

Cowgirl Marti Lee contributed this. She says, "This hoot of a recipe was from Rita McCafferty. She always made me smile with her quick wit!"

Ingredients are as follows:

1 cup butter
1 teaspoon salt
1 cup sugar
1 teaspoon baking soda
4 large eggs
Lemon juice
1 teaspoon baking powder
1 cup brown sugar
Nuts
1 or 2 quarts whiskey
1 cup dried fruit

Before you start, sample the whiskey to check for quality. Good, isn't it? Now go ahead. Select a large mixing bowl, measuring cup, etc. . . . Check the whiskey again as it must be just right to be sure whiskey is of the highest quality. Pour 1 level cup into a glass and drink it as fast as you can. Repeat. Now, with electric mixer beat 1 cup of butter in a fluffy bowl. Add 1 teaspoon of thugar and beat again. Meanwhile, make sure the whiskey is of the finest quality. Cry another tup. Open second quart of whiskey if necessary. Add 2 arge leggs, 2 cups of fried druit, and beat until high. If druit gets stuck in the beaters, just pry it loose with a drewscriver. Sample the whiskey again, thecking for tonsicity, then sift 2 cups of salt or anything. . . . It really doesn't matter. Sample the whiskey, sift ½ pint of lemon juice. Fold in chopped butter and strained nuts. Add 1 babblespoon of brown thugar or whatever clor you can find and mix well. Grease oven and turn cake pan to 350°F. Now pour the whole mess in the coven and ake. Check the whiskey again and bo to ged.

Boy's Best Dog Treats

There is no love quite like the love a Cowgirl has for her dog. It only makes sense that she would make these treats for that special four-footed and faithful friend. I make these for my rescued old gentleman border collie, "Boy."

Makes approximately 12 treats

> 2 eggs
> ½ cup canned pumpkin
> ½ teaspoon salt
> 2 tablespoons dry milk
> 2½ cups flour (Wheat is probably best for your dog's digestion.)
> Water

Preheat the oven to 350°F.

Blend the eggs and pumpkin together. Add salt, dry milk, and flour.

Add water as needed to make the dough somewhat workable. You will need to mix this with your hands because it is too stiff for an electric mixer. The dough should be dry and stiff; don't be concerned with crumbs being left in the bowl.

Roll dough to ½-inch thick. Cut into shapes, any shape. Boy is not particular.

Place 1 inch apart on an ungreased cookie sheet. Bake for 20 minutes on one side, then turn over and bake another 20 minutes.

JILL CHARLOTTE STANFORD

Saddlebag Pralines

Donna Higby, an Arizona Cowgirl friend, says, "Deciding on a recipe to share with other Cowgirls prompted me to think of one that could go in a saddlebag for a snack on the trail. This one packs nicely and can be a treat for your special horse. They are my go-to recipe to make for friends in the holiday season."

Makes approximately 1 pound

> 1 pound pecans (about 4 cups dry)
> 1 cup white sugar
> 1 teaspoon salt
> 1 teaspoon cinnamon
> 1 egg white

Preheat the oven to 275°F.

Place the pecans in a bowl. In a separate bowl, mix the sugar, salt, and cinnamon.

Beat the egg white (just fluff it up a bit) and pour over the pecans. Stir to coat. Sprinkle in the sugar mixture a little at a time, stirring to thoroughly coat the nuts.

Spread on a cookie sheet. Bake for 45 minutes, stirring every 15 minutes. Allow to cool … if you can wait!

Carrot Cake with
Whiskey Butter Frosting

Hold back two big carrots from your horse's treats and make this moist and good carrot cake. Top it with the Whiskey Butter Frosting and it's sure to be a hit!

Serves 8

1½ cups vegetable oil
2 cups sugar
4 eggs, well beaten
2 cups shredded carrots
1 cup crushed pineapple
2½ cups all-purpose flour
1 teaspoon baking soda
½ teaspoon salt
2 teaspoons cinnamon
1 cup chopped nuts

Preheat the oven to 350°F.

In a large bowl, mix all the ingredients together with a spoon.

Pour the batter into a 12 x 14-inch glass pan sprayed with a nonstick cooking spray. Bake for 35 to 40 minutes.

Cool completely before frosting with Whiskey Butter Frosting.

Whiskey Butter Frosting

    1 cup butter, softened
    1 teaspoon vanilla extract
    1 teaspoon milk
    3 cups confectioners' sugar
    ¼ cup whiskey (or more if you feel adventuresome!)

Cream the butter, then add the vanilla extract and milk.

Slowly add the confectioners' sugar.

Add the whiskey a tablespoon at a time and beat well.

Bonnie McCarroll

Bonnie McCarroll was born in 1897 on a cattle ranch at High Valley, near Boise, Idaho. Her name then was Mary Ellen "Dot" Treadwell. Raised by her mother, she learned to rope and ride. She married Frank McCarroll in 1914 (he was a rodeo performer, too) and adopted the nickname "Bonnie." In 1915, her first year of rodeo competition, McCarroll attracted national attention from a photograph taken of her being thrown from a horse named Silver at the Pendleton Round-Up. In 1922 she won two cowgirl bronc-riding championships at the Cheyenne, Wyoming, Frontier Days Rodeo and at the first rodeo held at Madison Square Garden in New York City. She performed before kings, queens, and President Calvin Coolidge in 1927. At the Pendleton Round-Up in 1929, she was badly injured and died ten days later in the hospital. She is buried in the Morris Hill Cemetery near Boise. There is often a bouquet of flowers on her grave.

Bonnie McCarroll

PHOTO COURTESY OF TED MOOMAW, OLD BUCKING HORSE MUSEUM

"I was badly bruised and shaken up, but then and there I made up my mind that I would never quit until I became a champion." —Bonnie McCarroll, bronc rider

Camping Out

Under the stars or in a fancy little vintage trailer "glamping," or just out in your own backyard, here are some tasty things to stir up over the fire.

PHOTO BY MARJORIE ROGERS

Campers Ham 'n' Cheese Omelet

A three-day campout with good friends and good horses at Sheep Springs Horse Camp in central Oregon remains one of my most treasured memories. The beauty of this recipe is that there is no tiresome cleanup—perfect for trips into the backcountry. You will be saddled up and out on the Windigo Trail in no time at all!

Depending on how many cowgirls will be enjoying this, be sure to have the correct amount of eggs, ham, and cheese at the ready!

  2 eggs per person
  1 quart-size Ziploc freezer bag (be sure to get the freezer type) per person
  ¼ cup (or a handful) diced ham per person
  ¼ cup (or a handful) crumbled cheddar cheese per person
  Tongs
  Dash of salt
  Dash of pepper

You already have a large pot of water on the boil over the campfire.

Each camper cracks her 2 eggs into her Ziploc bag and carefully scrambles the eggs with a fork. (Plastic works best.) Add the ham to the eggs in the bag.

Fold the bag to squeeze out the air and zip it shut. Double-check to make sure it is really zipped shut! Drop the bag into the boiling water and cook for 12 minutes.

Using the tongs, take the bag out of the water and open on a flat surface. Put the cheese in and zip it closed again. Put the bag back in the boiling water for 1 minute.

Using the tongs, remove the bag with your omelet inside. Slide the omelet out onto a paper plate, and season to taste with salt and pepper.

Sinful "Sinnamon" Rolls

With fresh, hot cinnamon rolls from your Dutch oven in the campfire and a fresh pot of coffee, you are ready to greet the day. You can easily cook canned cinnamon rolls in your Dutch oven when you're out on the trail. Just place one or two cans' worth of rolls in a Dutch oven lined with foil. Place the oven over hot coals, put the top on, and put more coals on top of it. Bake for about the same time as listed on the can for a skillet in the oven. Remove the rolls from the Dutch oven and frost with the can of frosting thoughtfully provided!

PHOTO BY MARJORIE ROGERS

Chicken Noodle in a Pot

This is from Jean Brown, an experienced backcountry packer who travels on her mule with a string of more mules behind her, in Idaho's rugged wild and scenic Middle Fork of the Salmon River. Her expertise is amazing.

Serves 8 hungry campers

Put all this in your Dutch oven:

> 1 canned whole chicken, undrained
> 1 (12-ounce) bag egg noodles
> 8 cups water
> 2 tablespoons dehydrated onion
> 2 tablespoons dehydrated celery
> 1 bay leaf
> Salt (or garlic salt) and pepper to taste

Fran's Campfire

Here's a good trick from camper Fran Rattay for cooking in a Dutch oven without a fire pit. More about Fran coming up.

You can Dutch oven cook on a picnic table using a metal pizza pan and three bricks. Arrange the bricks so that the pizza pan can sit securely on top, with the Dutch oven in place on top of a bed of coals. Start the coals on the pan, and when they are hot, transfer about two-thirds of them to the lid of the Dutch oven and leave about a third on the pizza pan. Rest the Dutch oven on the coals that remain on the pan and follow your recipe's cooking instructions. The bricks keep the heat from harming the table.

Jean says:"For a 9 x 6-inch Dutch oven (this is the best size to use because it is versatile), dig an 18 x 12-inch-deep hole next to your fire pit. Shovel about 6 inches of hot coals on the bottom of the hole you've dug and set the Dutch oven, with your meal prepared in it, on top. Put more hot coals around the sides and 4 inches of coals on the top. Now cover it all up with dirt. (You can also lay foil on top of the coals to hold in the heat.) Now saddle up and ride all day and when you come back, dinner is ready."

PHOTO BY JIM BROWN

Dutch Oven Meat Loaf

Jennifer Denison is the Senior Editor and Cowboy Culture Editor for *Western Horseman* magazine. When sharing this recipe with me, she said, "Growing up, both of my parents worked, so one of my chores was to start dinner each night when I got home from school. Meat loaf was a hearty favorite that produced leftovers, so I made it frequently and became known for my meat loaf recipe. Through the years, I have modified it. The past year, I started cooking in Dutch ovens over the fire and found my meat loaf recipe worked well in Dutch ovens. I hosted a Dutch-oven party this fall and people enjoyed learning about the traditional cooking method, and the meat loaf was a huge hit!"

PHOTO BY ROBIN JOHNSON

Serves 6

- ¾ cup milk
- 1 egg
- 2 cups chopped or torn corn tortillas
- 1 teaspoon salt
- 1 teaspoon pepper
- ½ teaspoon oregano
- ½ teaspoon dried basil
- ½ teaspoon chopped garlic
- 1 small onion, minced
- 1 green bell pepper, minced
- 2 tablespoons Worcestershire sauce, divided
- 1 pound lean ground beef, elk, or venison
- 1 pound Italian sausage
- 1 cup catsup
- 1 tablespoon brown sugar

Combine the milk, egg, tortilla pieces, spices, garlic, onion, bell pepper, 1 table-spoon Worcestershire sauce, and meat in a large bowl and mix well with your hands. Shape into a loaf and place into a 12-inch Dutch oven that has been coated with cooking spray or olive oil.

Bake in a 375°F oven for 1 to 1½ hours or until cooked throughout. If cooking outdoors, place meat loaf in a Dutch oven coated with olive oil or cooking spray and place over medium-heat coals. Add coals to the top of the Dutch oven and cook for an hour or so or until done throughout.

Combine catsup, brown sugar, and 1 tablespoon Worcestershire sauce in a pan and bring to a boil. Pour over meat loaf and bake 10 additional minutes.

Cheesy Corn Bread Casserole

Cowgirl Fran Rattay and her trusty trailer, "Kelly Sue," are members of Sisters on the Fly, a group of women who love nothing better than to hitch up and hit the road. When they get there, they like to cook outdoors. Fran says this recipe "never has any leftovers."

Serves 6

1 stick (½ cup) butter
½ medium onion, chopped
1 (8.5-ounce) box JIFFY corn bread mix
1 egg
1 cup grated sharp cheddar cheese
1 cup grated pepper jack cheese
1 (4-ounce) can fire-roasted chopped chiles
1 (15-ounce) can cream-style corn
1 (15-ounce) can whole-kernel corn, drained

Melt the butter in a Dutch oven and sauté the onion until it is transparent. Then mix in all the other ingredients.

To bake, place 8 to 10 coals underneath the Dutch oven, and 16 resting on top. Cook for 50 to 60 minutes.

Remove from the coals and let it "set" for 10 minutes before serving.

Iron Cowgirl Brownies

It is said that when you cook with iron utensils, a little of the iron leaches into your food, and that's a good thing! Women, especially Cowgirls, need iron in their diet. Here is a brownie recipe that you can bake in your well-seasoned iron skillet and feel full of vim and vigor with the results!

Serves 6–8

    1 cup sugar
    3 large eggs
    1 cup all-purpose flour
    ½ cup cocoa powder (Dutch-process is best!)
    ½ teaspoon salt
    ½ stick (¼ cup) unsalted butter
    ¼ cup heavy cream
    8 ounces semisweet chocolate chips

Preheat the oven to 350°F.

In a large bowl, stir together the sugar and eggs.

Sift the flour, cocoa, and salt into a separate large bowl.

In a medium cast-iron skillet, bring the butter and cream to a simmer over medium heat. Add the chocolate chips. Reduce the heat to medium-low. Cook, stirring constantly, until the chocolate has melted completely and the mixture is velvet smooth. Remove from the heat and let cool for 5 minutes.

Pour the chocolate mixture into the sugar mixture. Now stir in the flour mixture, then pour the whole batch back into the skillet.

Bake for 40 minutes. (If you like it "gooey," bake for 30 to 35 minutes.)

Serve the brownies directly from the skillet, with a dollop of whipped cream or vanilla ice cream on top.

Life loves to be taken by the lapel and told, "I'm with you kid. Let's go!"

—Maya Angelou

Any Berry Dutch Oven Cobbler

If you are lucky enough to go out into the wilderness, this is a dessert you won't regret taking along. Three ingredients only, making it easy to pack in the pack saddles when I took a pack trip to the Eagle Cap Wilderness in Oregon's Wallawa Mountains. Our camp cook shared this with me, and now I am sharing it with you. I wish I were going to be with you to enjoy it!

You will need a heavy, 6-quart Dutch oven with a lid that has a lip. Why? So you can shovel the hot coals on top to make it cook.

Serves 6 hungry packers

1 box white cake mix
2 cups of any canned berry pie filling. A mix of berries will do nicely (blueberries travel well), to which a cup of sugar has been added.
1 (12-ounce) can Sprite or 7UP

Empty the cake mix into a gallon-size Ziploc bag. Close securely.

Put the berries, washed (and hulled if need be), in another plastic Ziploc bag with the sugar and close securely.

Don't worry about the soda until you are going to open it—when you do, point it away from yourself and others, because it will be pretty fizzed up.

Start a good campfire and allow the wood to burn down to hot, glowing coals. Empty the berries into the Dutch oven.

Pour the soda right over the cake mix in its bag and mix it together. It will be lumpy but no matter.

It's pretty smart to put all your ingredients into another Ziploc bag big enough to hold all three. Closed securely, of course!

Pour the cake mix over the berries and then lower the Dutch oven into your hot coals. Shovel 20 coals on top (you don't have to be picky about this—just enough to cover the lid will do) and the rest are on the bottom.

Bake until the cake is golden brown, about 30 minutes.

Scrape off the top coals and lift up the Dutch oven from the bed of coals. Remove the lid to let it cool.

If you packed an 8-ounce can of evaporated milk for your campfire coffee in the morning, and it is cooling in the mountain stream or lake, so much the better! Pour some over this cobbler.

Stop By and Say Hello—Sources

You will want to fire up your laptop and stop in and say "howdy" to these fine Cowgirls and Cowboys I'd like to introduce you to. I consider them my friends. Tell 'em Jill sent you!

Old Bucking Horse Museum and Hall of Fame

What makes a Cowgirl look good on a bucking bronco? Why, the horse, of course! The horse is what will give you the points and therefore the purse.

Ted Moomaw comes from a family that provided all the great rodeos with their bucking stock. Find Ted on Facebook under Old Bucking Horse Museum— give him a "like" and learn all about the broncs that made rodeo. You can write to Ted, too, at Old Bucking Horse Museum, 330 Market Street, Baird, Texas 79504.

PHOTO COURTESY OF TED MOOMAW, OLD BUCKING HORSE MUSEUM

Jessica Hedges Cowboy Poetry

Jessica lives on a ranch with her husband, Sam, and young son, Quirt, but she's only a click away from telling you about her life on her blog, http://jessicahedgescowboypoetry.com/jessblog.cfm.

Twist N Ties

Meet Cindy Forbes, who lives on a ranch in Montana. She makes beautiful silk or polyester "Wild Rags." What's that, you ask? Wild Rags are Cowgirl scarves. Cindy chooses the pattern and color and ties it with her own distinctive knot or uses a silver scarf slide. I'm the proud owner of several from Cindy. She posts her fabrics and colors and patterns on Facebook. This has been my downfall. She accepts PayPal. Another downfall.

Don't know how to tie a Wild Rag? Here's how: www.coyotedroppings .com/2011/07/back-on-line-learn-to-tie-your-scarf.html?spref=fb.

Maid of the West

Longing to be a Rodeo Queen? Mary Lynn Duncan can make the perfect outfit for you. Hankering for a bridal dress in a period style, authentic down to the hand-sewn button holes? Yep, Maid of the West. She made me the most beautiful cuffs you ever did see, featuring my very own brand. If it walked on four hooves, Mary Lynn can whip it into something stylish. I call her the "female" Nudie—the man who made the amazing outfits for country-western stars. You can "like" Mary Lynn at www.facebook.com/maidofthewestranchwear.

Western Horseman Magazine

Western Horseman magazine began in 1936, which makes it one of the oldest horse magazines in the world. To glance back at the magazine's history is to survey much of the history of the horse industry in North America, because *Western Horseman* was there to champion the formation of breed associations and registries, research and record horse history, and publish accounts of the care, breeding, and use of horses through the decades.

Western Horseman has stayed true to its roots, and readers of the publication in 1936—those who are still with us—typically feel "at home" with the magazine today. Contemporary readers who run across those early issues find them fascinating. You will enjoy every page. Read more at www.western horseman.com.

I'd like to hear from you, too!
jillcharlotte.com
jill@jillcharlotte.com

Index

About the Author

Combine one part Cowgirl, one part cook, and one part writer who loves to share the stories of Cowgirls both past and present, ranch women, trick riders, and other "wild women," and you have a recipe for author Jill Charlotte Stanford. Growing up on Puget Sound in Washington State, Jill always knew she was a Cowgirl at heart. Summers spent horseback at a camp in central Oregon only cemented her determination. Her first horse, Buttons, opened up the world of Cowgirls for her, and she has never looked back. "I am the luckiest Cowgirl in the world," Jill says. "Writing about the women that I admire so much, sharing their stories and recipes,

PHOTO BY DAVID MENDENHALL

is like a dream come true. It is my hope that when you read this book, you will feel as if they invited you into their homes to enjoy their good food and hear some wonderful stories about their lives." Jill lives and writes in Sisters, Oregon. You can see all of her books at jillcharlotte.com.